图书在版编目（CIP）数据

李尔王：英汉对照 ／（英）莎士比亚（Shakespeare, W.）著；朱生豪译. -- 上海：上海世界图书出版公司，2014.1（2015.9 重印）

ISBN 978-7-5100-7167-6

Ⅰ．①李… Ⅱ．①莎… ②朱… Ⅲ．①英语－汉语－对照读物 ②悲剧－剧本－英国－中世纪 Ⅳ.①H319.4：I

中国版本图书馆 CIP 数据核字 (2013) 第 274962 号

李尔王

[英] 威廉·莎士比亚 著

朱生豪 译

上海世界图书出版公司 出版发行

上海市广中路 88 号

邮政编码 200083

北京中科印刷有限公司印刷

如发现印刷质量问题，请与印刷厂联系

（电质检科话：010-84897777）

各地新华书店经销

开本：880×1230　1/32　印张：10.5　字数：235 000

2015 年 9 月第 1 版第 2 次印刷

ISBN 978-7-5100-7167-6/H·1260

定价：26.80 元

http://www.wpcsh.com.cn

http://www.wpcsh.com

朱生豪译文卷

King Lear

李尔王

中英对照全译本

[英] 威廉·莎士比亚 著
William Shakespeare

朱生豪 译

世界图书出版公司
上海·西安·北京·广州

前　言

通过阅读文学名著学语言，是掌握英语的绝佳方法。既可接触原汁原味的英语，又能享受文学之美，一举两得，何乐不为？

对于喜欢阅读名著的读者，这是一个最好的时代，因为有成千上万的书可以选择；这又是一个不好的时代，因为在浩繁的卷帙中，很难找到适合自己的好书。

然而，你手中的这套丛书，值得你来信赖。

这套精选的中英对照名著全译丛书，未改编改写、未删节削减，且配有权威注释、部分书中还添加了精美插图。

要学语言、读好书，当读名著原文。如习武者切磋交流，同高手过招方能渐明其间奥妙，若一味在低端徘徊，终难登堂入室。积年流传的名著，就是书中"高手"。然而这个"高手"，却有真假之分。初读书时，常遇到一些挂了名著名家之名改写改编的版本，虽有助于了解基本情节，然而所得只是皮毛，你何曾真的就读过了那名著呢？一边是窖藏了50年的女儿红，一边是贴了女儿红标签的薄酒，那滋味，怎能一样？"朝闻道，夕死可矣。"人生短如朝露，当努力追求真正的美。

本套丛书还特别收录了十本朱生豪先生译著的莎士比亚戏剧，同样配有原著英文。朱生豪译本以"求于最大可能之范围内，保持原作之神韵"为宗旨，翻译考究、译笔流畅。他打破了莎士比亚写作的年代顺序，将戏剧分为喜剧、悲剧、史剧、杂剧四类编排，自成体系。本系列译文偶有异体字或旧译名，为方便读者理解，编者已一一加以注释。

读过本套丛书的原文全译，相信你会得书之真意、语言之精髓。

送君"开卷有益"之书，愿成文采斐然之人。

CONTENTS
目 录

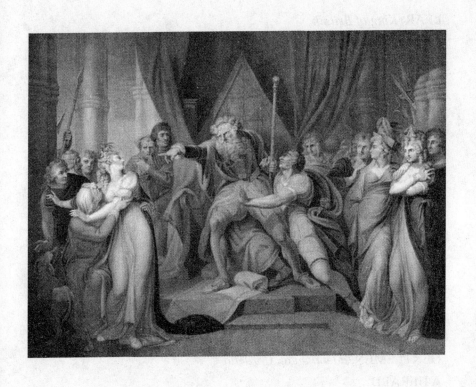

King Lear

DRAMATIS PERSONAE

LEAR, *King of Britain*

KING OF FRANCE

DUKE OF BURGUNDY

DUKE OF CORNWALL, *husband to Regan*

DUKE OF ALBANY, *husband to Goneril*

EARL OF KENT

EARL OF GLOSTER

EDGAR, *son to Gloster*

EDMUND, *bastard son to Gloster*

CURAN, *a courtier*

OLD MAN, *tenant to Gloster*

PHYSICIAN

FOOL

OSWALD, *steward to Goneril*

AN OFFICER, *employed by Edmund*

GENTLEMEN, *attendant on Cordelia*

A HERALD

SERVANTS *to Cornwall*

GONERIL, *daughter to Lear*

REGAN, *daughter to Lear*

CORDELIA, *daughter to Lear*

KNIGHTS attending on LEAR, OFFICERS, MESSENGERS, SOLDIERS, and ATTENDANTS

剧中人物

李尔，不列颠国王

法兰西国王

勃艮第公爵

康华尔公爵，里根的丈夫

奥本尼公爵，高纳里尔的丈夫

肯特伯爵

葛罗斯特伯爵

爱德伽，葛罗斯特之子

爱德蒙，葛罗斯特之庶子

克伦，朝士

老人，葛罗斯特的佃户

医生

弄人

奥斯华德，高纳里尔的管家

爱德蒙属下一军官

考狄利娅一侍臣

传令官

康华尔的众仆

高纳里尔，李尔之女

里根，李尔之女

考狄利娅，李尔之女

扈从李尔之骑士、军官、使者、兵士及侍从等

SCENE

Britain

地点

不列颠

ACT I   SCENE I

King Lear's Palace.
[*Enter Kent, Gloster, and Edmund.*]

EARL OF KENT.   I thought the King had more affected the Duke of Albany than Cornwall.

EARL OF GLOSTER.   It did always seem so to us; but now, in the division of the kingdom, it appears not which of the Dukes he values most, for equalities are so weighed that curiosity in neither can make choice of either's moiety.

EARL OF KENT.   Is not this your son, my lord?

EARL OF GLOSTER.   His breeding, sir, hath been at my charge. I have so often blushed to acknowledge him that now I am brazed to't.

EARL OF KENT.   I cannot conceive you.

EARL OF GLOSTER.   Sir, this young fellow's mother could; whereupon she grew round-wombed, and had indeed, sir, a son for her cradle ere she had a husband for her bed. Do you smell a fault?

EARL OF KENT.   I cannot wish the fault undone, the issue of it being so proper.

EARL OF GLOSTER.   But I have, sir, a son by order of law, some year elder than this, who yet is no dearer in my account. Though

第一幕　第一场

李尔王宫中大厅。

（肯特，葛罗斯特及爱德蒙上。）

肯特：　我想王上对于奥本尼公爵，比对于康华尔公爵更有好感。

葛罗斯特：　我们一向都觉得是这样；可是这次划分国土的时候，
　　　却看不出来他对这两位公爵有什么偏心；因为他分配得那么平
　　　均，无论他们怎样斤斤较量，都不能说对方比自己占了便宜。

肯特：　大人，这位是令郎吗？

葛罗斯特：　他是在我手里长大的；我常常不好意思承认他，可是
　　　现在惯了，也就不以为意啦。

肯特：　我不懂您的意思。

葛罗斯特：　伯爵，这个小子的母亲可心里明白；因此，不瞒您说，
　　　她还没有嫁人就大了肚子生下儿子来。您想这应该不应该？

肯特：　能够生下这样一个好儿子来，即使一时错误，也是可以原
　　　谅的。

葛罗斯特：　我还有一个合法的儿子，年纪比他大一岁，然而我还
　　　是喜欢他。这畜生虽然不等我的召唤，就自己莽莽撞撞来到这

this knave came something saucily into the world before he was sent for, yet was his mother fair, there was good sport at his making, and the whoreson must be acknowledged. – Do you know this noble gentleman, Edmund?

EDMUND.   No, my lord.

EARL OF GLOSTER.   My Lord of Kent: remember him hereafter as my honourable friend.

EDMUND.   My services to your lordship.

EARL OF KENT.   I must love you, and sue to know you better.

EDMUND.   Sir, I shall study deserving.

EARL OF GLOSTER.   He hath been out nine years, and away he shall again. Sound a sennet. The King is coming.

[*Sennet. Enter one bearing a coronet, King Lear, Cornwall, Albany, Goneril, Regan, Cordelia, and attendants.*]

KING LEAR.   Attend the lords of France and Burgundy, Gloster.

EARL OF GLOSTER.   I shall, my liege.

   [*Exeunt Gloster and Edmund.*]

KING LEAR.   Meantime we shall express our darker purpose.
   Give me the map there. Know we have divided
   In three our kingdom and 'tis our fast intent
   To shake all cares and business from our age,
   Conferring them on younger strengths while we
   Unburdened crawl toward death. Our son of Cornwall,

世上，可是他的母亲是个迷人的东西，我们在制造他的时候，曾经有过一场销魂的游戏，这孽种我不能不承认他。爱德蒙，你认识这位贵人吗？

爱德蒙：　　不认识，父亲。

葛罗斯特：　肯特伯爵；从此以后，你该记着他是我的尊贵的朋友。

爱德蒙：　　大人，我愿意为您效劳。

肯特：　　我一定喜欢你，希望我们以后能够常常见面。

爱德蒙：　　大人，我一定尽力报答您的垂爱。

葛罗斯特：　他已经在国外九年，不久还是要出去的。王上来了。

（喇叭奏花腔。李尔、康华尔、奥本尼、高纳里尔、里根、考狄利娅及侍从等上。）

李尔：　　葛罗斯特，你去招待招待法兰西国王和勃艮第公爵。

葛罗斯特：　是，陛下。（葛罗斯特、爱德蒙同下。）

李尔：　　现在我要向你们说明我的心事。把那地图给我。告诉你们吧，我已经把我的国土划成三部分；我因为自己年纪老了，决心摆脱一切世务的牵萦，把责任交卸给年轻力壮之人，让自己松一松肩，好安安心心地等死。康华尔贤婿，还有同样是我心爱的奥本尼贤婿，为了预防他日的争执，我想还是趁现在把我的几个女儿的嫁妆当众分配清楚。法兰西和勃艮第两位君主正在竞争我的

And you, our no less loving son of Albany,

We have this hour a constant will to publish

Our daughters' several dowers, that future strife

May be prevented now. The princes, France and Burgundy,

Great rivals in our youngest daughter's love,

Long in our court have made their amorous sojourn,

And here are to be answered. Tell me, my daughters

Since now we will divest us both of rule,

Interest of territory, cares of state,

Which of you shall we say doth love us most?

That we our largest bounty may extend

Where nature doth with merit challenge. Goneril,

Our eldest-born, speak first.

GONERIL. Sir, I love you more than words can wield the matter;

Dearer than eyesight, space, and liberty;

Beyond what can be valued, rich or rare;

No less than life, with grace, health, beauty, honour;

As much as child e'er loved, or father found;

A love that makes breath poor, and speech unable.

Beyond all manner of so much I love you.

CORDELIA. [*Aside.*] What shall Cordelia speak? Love, and be silent.

KING LEAR. Of all these bounds, even from this line to this,

With shadowy forests and with champains riched,

With plenteous rivers and wide-skirted meads,

We make thee lady. To thine and Albany's issue.

Be this perpetual. – What says our second daughter,

小女儿的爱情，他们为了求婚而住在我们宫廷里，也已经有好多时候了，现在他们就可以得到答复。孩子们，在我还没有把我的政权、领土和国事的重任全部放弃以前，告诉我，你们中间哪一个人最爱我？我要看看谁最有孝心，最有贤德，我就给她最大的恩惠。高纳里尔，我的大女儿，你先说。

高纳里尔：　父亲，我对您的爱，不是言语所能表达的；我爱您胜过自己的眼睛、整个的空间和广大的自由；超越一切可以估价的贵重稀有的事物；不亚于赋有淑德、健康、美貌和荣誉的生命；不曾有一个儿女这样爱过他的父亲，也不曾有一个父亲这样被他的儿女所爱；这一种爱可以使唇舌无能为力，辩才失去效用；我爱您是不可以数量计算的。

考狄利娅：　（旁白）考狄利娅应该怎么好呢？默默地爱着吧。

李尔：　在这些疆界以内，从这一条线起，直到这一条界线为止，所有一切浓密的森林、膏腴的平原、富庶的河流、广大的牧场，都要奉你为它们的女主人；这一块土地永远为你和奥本尼的子孙所保有。我的二女儿，最亲爱的里根，康华尔的夫人，你怎么说？

Our dearest Regan, wife to Cornwall? Speak.

REGAN.　　Sir, I am made Of the selfsame metal that my sister is,

And prize me at her worth. my true heart

I find she names my very deed of love;

Only she comes too short, that I profess

Myself an enemy to all other joys

Which the most precious square of sense possesses,

And find I am alone felicitate

In your dear Highness' love.

CORDELIA.　　[*Aside.*] Then poor Cordelia!

And yet not so; since I am sure my love's

More richer than my tongue.

KING LEAR.　　To thee and thine hereditary ever

Remain this ample third of our fair kingdom,

No less in space, validity, and pleasure

Than that conferred on Goneril. – Now, our joy,

Although the last, not least; to whose young love

The vines of France. and milk of Burgundy

Strive to be interest; what can you say to draw

A third more opulent than your sisters? Speak.

CORDELIA.　　Nothing, my lord.

KING LEAR.　　Nothing?

CORDELIA.　　Nothing.

KING LEAR.　　Nothing can come of nothing. Speak again.

CORDELIA.　　Unhappy that I am, I cannot heave

My heart into my mouth. I love your Majesty

里根：　　我跟姐姐具有同样的品质，您凭着她就可以判断我。在我的真心之中，我觉得她刚才所说的话，正是我爱您的实际的情形，可是她还不能充分说明我的心理：我厌弃一切凡是敏锐的知觉所能感受到的快乐，只有爱您才是我的无上的幸福。

考狄利娅：　　（旁白）那么，考狄利娅，你只好自安于贫穷了！可是我并不贫穷，因为我深信我的爱心比我的口才更富有。

李尔：　　这一块从我们这美好的王国中划分出来的三分之一的沃壤，是你和你的子孙永远世袭的产业，和高纳里尔所得到的一份同样广大、同样富庶，也同样佳美。现在，我的宝贝，虽然是最后的一个，却并非最不在我的心头；法兰西的葡萄和勃艮第的乳酪都在竞争你的青春之爱；你有些什么话，可以换到一份比你的两个姐姐更富庶的土地？说吧。

考狄利娅：　　父亲，我没有话说。
李尔：　　没有？
考狄利娅：　　没有。
李尔：　　没有只能换到没有；重新说过。
考狄利娅：　　我是个笨拙的人，不会把我的心涌上我的嘴里；我爱您只是按照我的名分，一分不多，一分不少。

According to my bond; no more nor less.

KING LEAR.   How, how, Cordelia? Mend your speech a little,

Lest it may mar your fortunes.

CORDELIA.   Good my lord,

You have begot me, bred me, loved me; I

Return those duties back as are right fit,

Obey you, love you, and most honour you.

Why have my sisters husbands, if they say

They love you all? Haply, when I shall wed,

That lord whose hand must take my plight shall carry

Half my love with him, half my care and duty.

Sure I shall never marry like my sisters,

To love my father all.

KING LEAR.   But goes thy heart with this?

CORDELIA.   Ay, good my lord.

KING LEAR.   So young, and so untender?

CORDELIA.   So young, my lord, and true.

KING LEAR.   Let it be so! thy truth then be thy dower!

For, by the sacred radiance of the sun,

The mysteries of Hecate and the night;

By all the operation of the orbs

From whom we do exist and cease to be;

Here I disclaim all my paternal care,

Propinquity and property of blood,

And as a stranger to my heart and me

Hold thee from this for ever. The barbarous Scythian,

李尔： 怎么，考狄利娅！把你的话修正修正，否则你要毁坏你自己的命运了。

考狄利娅： 父亲，您生下我来，把我教养成人，爱惜我、厚待我；我受到您这样的恩德，只有恪尽我的责任，服从您、爱您、敬重您。我的姐姐们要是用她们整个的心来爱您，那么她们为什么要嫁人呢？要是我有一天出嫁了，那接受我的忠诚的誓约的丈夫，将要得到我的一半的爱、我的一半的关心和责任；假如我只爱我的父亲，我一定不会像我的两个姐姐一样再去嫁人的。

李尔： 你这些话果然是从心里说出来的吗？

考狄利娅： 是的，父亲。

李尔： 年纪这样小，却这样没有良心吗？

考狄利娅： 父亲，我年纪虽小，我的心却是忠实的。

李尔： 好，那么让你的忠实做你的嫁妆吧。凭着太阳神圣的光辉，凭着黑夜的神秘，凭着主宰人类生死的星球的运行，我发誓从现在起，永远和你断绝一切父女之情和血缘亲属的关系，把你当做一个路人看待。啖食自己儿女的生番，比起你，我的旧日的女儿来，也不会更令我憎恨。

Or he that makes his generation messes

To gorge his appetite, shall to my bosom

Be as well neighboured, pitied, and relieved,

As thou my sometime daughter.

EARL OF KENT.　Good my liege –

KING LEAR.　Peace, Kent!

Come not between the dragon and his wrath.

I loved her most, and thought to set my rest

On her kind nursery. – Hence and avoid my sight! –

So be my grave my peace as here I give

Her father's heart from her!

Call France! Who stirs? Call Burgundy! Cornwall and Albany,

With my two daughters' dowers digest this third;

Let pride, which she calls plainness, marry her.

I do invest you jointly in my power,

Preeminence, and all the large effects

That troop with majesty. Ourself, by monthly course,

With reservation of an hundred knights,

By you to be sustained, shall our abode

Make with you by due turns. Only we still retain

The name, and all th' additions to a king.

The sway, Revenue, execution of the rest,

Beloved sons, be yours; which to confirm,

This coronet part betwixt you.

EARL OF KENT.　Royal Lear,

Whom I have ever honoured as my king,

肯特： 陛下——

李尔： 闭嘴，肯特！不要来批怒龙的逆鳞。她是我最爱的一个，
我本来想要在她的殷勤看护之下，终养我的天年。去，不要让
我看见你的脸！让坟墓做我安息的眠床吧，我从此割断对她的
天伦的慈爱了！叫法兰西王来！都是死人吗？叫勃艮第来！康
华尔，奥本尼，你们已经分到我的两个女儿的嫁妆，现在把我
第三个女儿那一份也拿去分了吧；让骄傲——她自己所称为坦
白的——替她找一个丈夫。我把我的威力、特权和一切君主的
尊荣一起给了你们。我自己只保留一百名骑士，在你们两人的
地方按月轮流居住，由你们负责供养。除了国王的名义和尊号
以外，所有行政的大权、国库的收入和大小事务的处理，完全
交在你们手里；为了证实我的话，两位贤婿，我赐给你们这一
顶宝冠，归你们两人共同保有。

肯特： 尊严的李尔，我一向敬重您像敬重我的君王，爱您像爱我
的父亲，跟随您像跟随我的主人，在我的祈祷之中，我总把您

Loved as my father, as my master followed,

As my great patron thought on in my prayers –

KING LEAR.   The bow is bent and drawn; make from the shaft.

EARL OF KENT.   Let it fall rather, though the fork invade

The region of my heart! Be Kent unmannerly

When Lear is mad. What wouldst thou do, old man?

Think'st thou that duty shall have dread to speak

When power to flattery bows? To plainness honour's bound

When majesty falls to folly. Reverse thy doom;

And in thy best consideration check

This hideous rashness. Answer my life my judgment,

Thy youngest daughter does not love thee least,

Nor are those empty-hearted whose low sound

Reverb no hollowness.

KING LEAR.   Kent, on thy life, no more!

EARL OF KENT.   My life I never held but as a pawn

To wage against thine enemies; nor fear to lose it,

Thy safety being the motive.

KING LEAR.   Out of my sight!

EARL OF KENT.   See better, Lear, and let me still remain

The true blank of thine eye.

KING LEAR.   Now by Apollo –

EARL OF KENT.   Now by Apollo, King,

Thou swear'st thy gods in vain.

KING LEAR.   O vassal! miscreant!

[*Laying his hand on his sword.*]

当做我的伟大的恩主——

李尔：　弓已经弯好拉满，你留心躲开箭锋吧。

肯特：　让它落下来吧，即使箭镞会刺进我的心里。李尔发了疯，肯特也只好不顾礼貌了。你究竟要怎样，老头儿？你以为有权有位的人向谄媚者低头，尽忠守职的臣僚就不敢说话了吗？君主不顾自己的尊严，干下了愚蠢的事情，在朝的端人正士只好直言极谏。保留你的权力，仔细考虑一下你的举措，收回这种鲁莽灭裂的成命。你的小女儿并不是最不孝顺你；有人不会口若悬河，说得天花乱坠，可并不就是无情无义。我的判断要是有错，你尽管取我的命。

李尔：　肯特，你要是想活命，赶快闭住你的嘴。

肯特：　我的生命本来是预备向你的仇敌抛掷的；为了你的安全，我也不怕把它失去。

李尔：　走开，不要让我看见你！

肯特：　瞧明白一些，李尔；还是让我像箭垛上的红心一般永远站在你的眼前吧。

李尔：　凭着阿波罗起誓——

肯特：　凭着阿波罗，老王，你向神明发誓也是没用的。

李尔：　啊，可恶的奴才！（以手按剑。）

DUKES OF ALBANY and CORNWALL.　　Dear sir, forbear!

EARL OF KENT.　　Do;

> Kill thy physician, and the fee bestow
>
> Upon the foul disease. Revoke thy gift,
>
> Or, whilst I can vent clamour from my throat,
>
> I'll tell thee thou dost evil.

KING LEAR.　　Hear me, recreant!

> On thine allegiance, hear me!
>
> Since thou hast sought to make us break our vow –
>
> Which we durst never yet – and with strained pride
>
> To come between our sentence and our power, –
>
> Which nor our nature nor our place can bear, –
>
> Our potency made good, take thy reward.
>
> Five days we do allot thee for provision
>
> To shield thee from diseases of the world,
>
> And on the sixth to turn thy hated back
>
> Upon our kingdom. If, on the tenth day following,
>
> Thy banished trunk be found in our dominions,
>
> The moment is thy death. Away! By Jupiter,
>
> This shall not be revoked.

EARL OF KENT.　　Fare thee well, King. Since thus thou wilt appear,

> Freedom lives hence, and banishment is here.
>
> [*To Cordelia.*] The gods to their dear shelter take thee, maid,
>
> That justly think'st and hast most rightly said!
>
> [*To Regan and Goneril.*] And your large speeches may your deeds
>
> approve,

奥本尼、康华尔：　陛下请息怒。

肯特：　好，杀了你的医生，把你的恶病养得一天比一天厉害吧。
　　　　赶快撤销你的分土授国的原议；否则只要我的喉舌尚在，我就
　　　　要大声疾呼，告诉你你做了错事啦。

李尔：　听着，逆贼！你给我按照做臣子的道理，好生听着！你想
　　　　要煽动我毁弃我的不容更改的誓言，凭着你的不法的趑趄，对
　　　　我的命令和权力妄加阻挠，这一种目无君上的态度，使我忍无
　　　　可忍；为了维持王命的尊严，不能不给你应得的处分。我现在
　　　　宽容你五天的时间，让你预备些应用的衣服食物，免得受饥寒
　　　　的痛苦；在第六天上，你那可憎的身体必须离开我的国境；要
　　　　是在此后十天之内，我们的领土上再发现了你的踪迹，那时候
　　　　就要把你当场处死。去！凭着朱庇特发誓，这一个判决是无可
　　　　改移的。

肯特：　再会，国王；你既不知悔改，
　　　　囚笼里也没有自由存在。
　　　　（向考狄利娅）姑娘，自有神明为你照应：
　　　　你心地纯洁，说话真诚！
　　　　（向里根、高纳里尔）愿你们的夸口变成实事，

That good effects may spring from words of love.

Thus Kent, O princes, bids you all adieu;

He'll shape his old course in a country new.

[*Exit.*]

[*Flourish. Enter Gloster, with France and Burgundy; Attendants.*]

EARL OF GLOSTER.　Here's France and Burgundy, my noble lord.

KING LEAR.　My Lord of Burgundy,

We first address toward you, who with this king

Hath rivalled for our daughter. What in the least

Will you require in present dower with her,

Or cease your quest of love?

DUKE OF BURGUNDY.　Most royal Majesty,

I crave no more than hath your Highness offered,

Nor will you tender less.

KING LEAR.　Right noble Burgundy,

When she was dear to us, we did hold her so;

But now her price is fall'n. Sir, there she stands.

If aught within that little seeming substance,

Or all of it, with our displeasure pieced,

And nothing more, may fitly like your Grace,

She's there, and she is yours.

DUKE OF BURGUNDY.　I know no answer.

KING LEAR.　Will you, with those infirmities she owes,

Unfriended, new adopted to our hate,

假树上会结下真的果子

各位王子，肯特从此远去；

到新的国土走他的旧路。（下。）

（喇叭奏花腔。葛罗斯特偕法兰西王、勃艮第及侍从等重上。）

葛罗斯特：　陛下，法兰西国王和勃艮第公爵来了。

李尔：　勃艮第公爵，您跟这位国王都是来向我的女儿求婚的，现在我先问您：您希望她至少要有多少陪嫁的奁资，否则宁愿放弃对她的追求？

勃艮第：　陛下，照着您所已经答应的数目，我就很满足了；想来您也不会再吝惜的。

李尔：　尊贵的勃艮第，当她为我所宠爱的时候，我是把她看得非常珍重的，可是现在她的价格已经跌落了。公爵，您瞧她站在那儿，一个小小的东西，要是除了我的憎恨以外，我什么都不给她，而您仍然觉得她有使您喜欢的地方，或者您觉得她整个儿都能使您满意，那么她就在那儿，您把她带去好了。

勃艮第：　我不知道怎样回答。

李尔：　像她这样一个一无可取的女孩子，没有亲友的照顾，新近遭到我的憎恨，诅咒是她的嫁妆，我已经立誓和她断绝关系了，

Dowered with our curse, and strangered with our oath,

Take her, or leave her?

DUKE OF BURGUNDY.　Pardon me, royal sir.

Election makes not up on such conditions

KING LEAR.　Then leave her, sir; for, by the power that made me,

I tell you all her wealth. [*To France*] For you, great King,

I would not from your love make such a stray

To match you where I hate; therefore beseech you

T' avert your liking a more worthier way

Than on a wretch whom nature is ashamed

Almost t' acknowledge hers. quest of love?

KING OF FRANCE.　This is most strange,

That she that even but now was your best object,

The argument of your praise, balm of your age,

Most best, most dearest, should in this trice of time

Commit a thing so monstrous to dismantle

So many folds of favour. Sure her offence

Must be of such unnatural degree

That monsters it, or your fore-vouched affection

Fallen into taint; which to believe of her

Must be a faith that reason without miracle

Should never plant in me.

CORDELIA.　I yet beseech your Majesty,

If for I want that glib and oily art

To speak and purpose not, since what I well intend,

I'll do't before I speak – that you make known

您还是愿意娶她呢，还是愿意把她放弃？

勃艮第：　恕我，陛下；在这种条件之下，决定取舍是一件很为难
　　　　的事。

李尔：　那么放弃她吧，公爵；凭着赋予我生命的神明起誓，我已
　　　　经告诉您她的全部价值了。(向法兰西王)至于您，伟大的国王，
　　　　为了重视你、我的友谊，我断不愿把一个我所憎恶的人匹配给
　　　　您；所以请您还是丢开了这一个为天地所不容的贱人，另外去
　　　　找寻佳偶吧。

法兰西王：　这太奇怪了，她刚才还是您的眼中的珍宝、您的赞美
　　　　的题目、您的老年的安慰、您的最好、最心爱的人儿，怎么一
　　　　转瞬间，就会干下这么一件罪大恶极的行为，丧失了您的深恩
　　　　厚爱！她的罪恶倘不是超乎寻常，您的爱心绝不会变得这样厉
　　　　害；可是除非那是一桩奇迹，我无论如何不相信她会干那样的
　　　　事。

考狄利娅：　陛下，我只是因为缺少娓娓动人的口才，不会讲一些
　　　　违心的言语，凡是我心里想到的事情，我总不愿在没有把它实
　　　　行以前就放在嘴里宣扬；要是您因此而恼我，我必须请求您让
　　　　世人知道，我所以失去您的欢心的原因，并不是什么丑恶的污

It is no vicious blot, murther, or foulness,

No unchaste action or dishonoured step,

That hath deprived me of your grace and favour;

But even for want of that for which I am richer –

A still-soliciting eye, and such a tongue

As I am glad I have not, though not to have it

Hath lost me in your liking.

KING LEAR.   Better thou

Hadst not been born than not t' have pleased me better.

KING OF FRANCE.   Is it but this – a tardiness in nature

Which often leaves the history unspoken

That it intends to do? My Lord of Burgundy,

What say you to the lady? Love's not love

When it is mingled with regards that stands

Aloof from th' entire point. Will you have her?

She is herself a dowry.

DUKE OF BURGUNDY.   Royal Lear,

Give but that portion which yourself proposed,

And here I take Cordelia by the hand,

Duchess of Burgundy.

KING LEAR.   Nothing! I have sworn; I am firm.

DUKE OF BURGUNDY.   I am sorry then you have so lost a father

That you must lose a husband.

CORDELIA.   Peace be with Burgundy!

Since that respects of fortune are his love,

I shall not be his wife.

点、淫邪的行动，或是不名誉的举止；只是因为我缺少像人家那样的一双献媚求恩的眼睛，一条我所认为可耻的善于逢迎的舌头，虽然没有了这些使我不能再受您的宠爱，可是惟其如此，却使我格外尊重我自己的人格。

李尔：　像你这样不能在我面前曲意承欢，还不如当初没有生下你来的好。

法兰西王：　只是为了这一个原因吗？为了生性不肯有话便说，不肯把心里想做到的出之于口？勃艮第公爵，您对于这位公主意下如何？爱情里面要是掺杂了和它本身无关的算计，那就不是真的爱情。您愿不愿意娶她？她自己就是一注无价的嫁妆。

勃艮第：　尊严的李尔，只要把您原来已经允许过的那一份嫁妆给我，我现在就可以使考狄利娅成为勃艮第公爵的夫人。

李尔：　我什么都不给；我已经发过誓，再也不能挽回了。

勃艮第：　那么抱歉得很，您已经失去一个父亲，现在必须再失去一个丈夫了。

考狄利娅：　愿勃艮第平安！他所爱的既然只是财产，我也不愿做他的妻子。

KING OF FRANCE.   Fairest Cordelia, that art most rich, being poor;

Most choice, forsaken; and most loved, despised!

Thee and thy virtues here I seize upon.

Be it lawful I take up what's cast away.

Gods, gods! 'tis strange that from their cold'st neglect

My love should kindle to inflamed respect.

Thy dowerless daughter, King, thrown to my chance,

Is queen of us, of ours, and our fair France.

Not all the dukes in wat'rish Burgundy

Can buy this unprized precious maid of me.

Bid them farewell, Cordelia, though unkind.

Thou losest here, a better where to find.

KING LEAR.   Thou hast her, France; let her be thine; for we

Have no such daughter, nor shall ever see

That face of hers again. Therefore be gone

Without our grace, our love, our benison.

Come, noble Burgundy.

[*Flourish. Exeunt Lear, Burgundy, Cornwall, Albany, Gloster and Attendants.*]

KING OF FRANCE.   Bid farewell to your sisters.

CORDELIA.   The jewels of our father, with washed eyes

Cordelia leaves you. I know you what you are;

And, like a sister, am most loath to call

Your faults as they are named. Use well our father.

法兰西王：　　最美丽的考狄利娅！你因为贫穷，所以是最富有的；
　　　　　你因为被遗弃，所以是最可宝贵的；你因为遭人轻视，所以最
　　　　　蒙我的怜爱。我现在把你和你的美德一起攞在我的手里；人弃
　　　　　我取是法理上所许可的。天啊天！想不到他们的冷酷的蔑视，
　　　　　却会激起我热烈的敬爱。陛下，您的没有嫁妆的女儿被抛在一
　　　　　边，正好成全我的良缘；她现在是我的分享荣华的王后，法兰
　　　　　西全国的女主人了；沼泽之邦的勃艮第所有的公爵，都不能从
　　　　　我手里买去这一个无价之宝的女郎。考狄利娅，向他们告别吧，
　　　　　虽然他们是这样冷酷无情；你抛弃了故国，将要得到一个更好
　　　　　的家乡。

李尔：　　你带了她去吧，法兰西王；她是你的，我没有这样的女儿，
　　　　　也再不要看见她的脸，去吧，你们不要想得到我的恩宠和祝福。
　　　　　来，尊贵的勃艮第公爵。

（喇叭奏花腔。李尔、勃艮第、康华尔、奥本尼、葛罗斯特及侍从
等同下。）

法兰西王：　　向你的两位姐姐告别吧。
考狄利娅：　　父亲眼中的两颗宝玉，考狄利娅用泪洗过的眼睛向你
　　　　　们告别。我知道你们是怎样的人；因为碍着姊妹的情分，我不
　　　　　愿直言指斥你们的错处。好好对待父亲；你们自己说是孝敬他
　　　　　的，我把他托付给你们了。可是，唉！要是我没有失去他的欢

To your professed bosoms I commit him;

But yet, alas, stood I within his grace,

I would prefer him to a better place!

So farewell to you both.

REGAN.   Prescribe not us our duties.

GONERIL.   Let your study

Be to content your lord, who hath received you

At fortune's alms. You have obedience scanted,

And well are worth the want that you have wanted.

CORDELIA.   Time shall unfold what plighted cunning hides.

Who cover faults, at last shame them derides.

Well may you prosper!

KING OF FRANCE.   Come, my fair Cordelia.

[*Exeunt France and Cordelia.*]

GONERIL.   Sister, it is not little I have to say of what most nearly

appertains to us both. I think our father will hence to-night.

REGAN   That's most certain, and with you; next month with us.

GONERIL.   You see how full of changes his age is. The observation

we have made of it hath not been little. He always loved our sister

most, and with what poor judgment he hath now cast her off

appears too grossly.

REGAN.   Tis the infirmity of his age; yet he hath ever but slenderly

known himself.

GONERIL.   The best and soundest of his time hath been but rash; then

must we look to receive from his age, not alone the imperfections

of long-engraffed condition, but therewithal the

心，我一定不让他依赖你们的照顾。再会了，两位姐姐。

里根：　我们用不着你教训。

高纳里尔：　你还是去小心侍候你的丈夫吧，命运的慈悲把你交在他的手里；你自己忤逆不孝，今天空手跟了汉子去也是活该。

考狄利娅：　总有一天，深藏的奸诈会渐渐显出它的原形；罪恶虽然可以掩饰一时，免不了最后出乖露丑。愿你们幸福！

法兰西王：　来，我美丽的考狄利娅。（法兰西王、考狄利娅同下。）

高纳里尔：　妹妹，我有许多对我们两人有切身关系的话必须跟你谈谈。我想我们的父亲今晚就要离开此地。

里根：　那是十分确定的事，他要住到你们那儿去；下个月他就要跟我们住在一起了。

高纳里尔：　你瞧他现在年纪老了，他的脾气多么变化不定；我们已经屡次注意到他的行为的乖僻了。他一向都是最爱我们妹妹的，现在他凭着一时的气恼就把她撵走，这就可以见得他是多么糊涂。

里根：　这是他老年的昏悖；可是他向来就是这样喜怒无常的。

高纳里尔：　他年轻的时候性子就很暴躁，现在他任性惯了，再加上老年人刚愎自用的怪脾气，看来我们只好准备受他的气了。

unruly waywardness that infirm and choleric years bring with them.

REGAN.　Such unconstant starts are we like to have from him as this of Kent's banishment.

GONERIL.　There is further compliment of leave-taking between France and him. Pray you let's hit together. If our father carry authority with such dispositions as he bears, this last surrender of his will but offend us.

REGAN.　We shall further think on't.

GONERIL.　We must do something, and i' th' heat.

　　[*Exeunt.*]

里根：　他把肯特也放逐了；谁知道他心里一不高兴起来，不会用同样的手段对付我们？

高纳里尔：　法兰西王辞行回国，跟他还有一番礼仪上的应酬。让我们同心合力，决定一个方策；要是我们的父亲顺着他这种脾气滥施威权起来，这一次的让国对于我们未必有什么好处。

里根：　我们还要仔细考虑一下。

高纳里尔：　我们必须趁早想个办法。（同下。）

ACT I SCENE II

The Earl of Gloster's Castle.
[Enter Edmund, with a letter.]

EDMUND.   Thou, Nature, art my goddess; to thy law
       My services are bound. Wherefore should I
       Stand in the plague of custom, and permit
       The curiosity of nations to deprive me,
       For that I am some twelve or fourteen moonshines
       Lag of a brother? Why bastard? wherefore base?
       When my dimensions are as well compact,
       My mind as generous, and my shape as true,
       As honest madam's issue? Why brand they us
       With base? with baseness? bastardy? base, base?
       Who, in the lusty stealth of nature, take
       More composition and fierce quality
       Than doth, within a dull, stale, tired bed,
       Go to th' creating a whole tribe of fops
       Got 'tween asleep and wake? Well then,
       Legitimate Edgar, I must have your land.
       Our father's love is to the bastard Edmund
       As to th' legitimate. Fine word – legitimate!

第一幕　第二场

葛罗斯特伯爵城堡中的厅堂。

（爱德蒙持信上。）

爱德蒙：　　大自然，你是我的女神，我愿意在你的法律之前俯首听
命。为什么我要受世俗的排挤，让世人的歧视剥夺我的应享的
权利，只因为我比一个哥哥迟生了一年或是十四个月？为什么
他们要叫我私生子？为什么我比人家卑贱？我的壮健的体格、
我的慷慨的精神、我的端正的容貌，哪一点比不上正经女人生
下的儿子？为什么他们要给我加上庶出、贱种、私生子的恶名？
贱种，贱种；贱种？难道在热烈兴奋的奸情里，得天地精华、
父母元气而生下的孩子，倒不及拥着一个毫无欢趣的老婆，在
半睡半醒之间制造出来的那一批蠢货？好，合法的爱德伽，我
一定要得到你的土地；我们的父亲喜欢他的私生子爱德蒙，正
像他喜欢他的合法的嫡子一样。好听的名词，"合法"！好，
我的合法的哥哥，要是这封信发生效力，我的计策能够成功，
瞧着吧，庶出的爱德蒙将要把合法的嫡子压在他的下面——那
时候我可要扬眉吐气啦。神啊，帮助帮助私生子吧！

Well, my legitimate, if this letter speed,

And my invention thrive, Edmund the base

Shall top th' legitimate. I grow; I prosper.

Now, gods, stand up for bastards!

[*Enter Gloster.*]

EARL OF GLOSTER.   Kent banished thus? and France in choler parted?

And the King gone to-night? Prescribed his power?

Confined to exhibition? All this done

Upon the gad? Edmund, how now? What news?

EDMUND.   So please your lordship, none.

[*Puts up the letter.*]

EARL OF GLOSTER.   Why so earnestly seek you to put up that letter?

EDMUND.   I know no news, my lord.

EARL OF GLOSTER.   What paper were you reading?

EDMUND.   Nothing, my lord.

EARL OF GLOSTER.   No? What needed then that terrible dispatch of it into your pocket? The quality of nothing hath not such need to hide itself. Let's see. Come, if it be nothing, I shall not need spectacles.

EDMUND.   I beseech you, sir, pardon me. It is a letter from my brother that I have not all o'er-read; and for so much as I have perused, I find it not fit for your o'er-looking.

（葛罗斯特上。）

葛罗斯特：　肯特就这样放逐了！法兰西王盛怒而去；王上昨晚又走了！他的权力全部交出，依靠他的女儿过活！这些事情都在匆促中决定，不曾经过丝毫的考虑！爱德蒙，怎么！有什么消息？

爱德蒙：　禀父亲，没有什么消息。（藏信。）

葛罗斯特：　你为什么急急忙忙地把那封信藏起来？

爱德蒙：　我不知道有什么消息，父亲。

葛罗斯特：　你读的是什么信？

爱德蒙：　没有什么，父亲。

葛罗斯特：　没有什么？那么你为什么慌慌张张地把它塞进你的衣袋里去？既然没有什么，何必藏起来？来，给我看；要是那上面没有什么话，我也可以不用戴眼镜。

爱德蒙：　父亲，请您原谅我；这是我哥哥写给我的一封信，我还没有把它读完，照我所已经读到的一部分看起来，我想还是不要让您看见的好。

EARL OF GLOSTER.   Give me the letter, sir.

EDMUND.   I shall offend, either to detain or give it. The contents, as in part I understand them, are to blame.

EARL OF GLOSTER.   Let's see, let's see!

EDMUND.   I hope, for my brother's justification, he wrote this but as an essay or taste of my virtue.

EARL OF GLOSTER.   [*Reads.*] This policy and reverence of age makes the world bitter to the best of our times keeps our fortunes from us till our oldness cannot relish them. I begin to find an idle and fond bondage in the oppression of aged tyranny, who sways, not as it hath power, but as it is suffered. Come to me, that of this I may speak more. If our father would sleep till I waked him, you should enjoy half his revenue for ever, and live the beloved of your brother, Edgar. Hum! Conspiracy? Sleep till I waked him, you should enjoy half his revenue. My son Edgar! Had he a hand to write this? a heart and brain to breed it in? When came this to you? Who brought it?

EDMUND.   It was not brought me, my lord: there's the cunning of it. I found it thrown in at the casement of my closet.

EARL OF GLOSTER.   You know the character to be your brother's?

EDMUND.   If the matter were good, my lord, I durst swear it were his; but in respect of that, I would fain think it were not.

EARL OF GLOSTER.   It is his.

EDMUND.   It is his hand, my lord; but I hope his heart is not in the contents.

EARL OF GLOSTER.   Hath he never before sounded you in this

葛罗斯特：　　把信给我。

爱德蒙：　　不给您看您要恼我，给您看了您又要动怒。哥哥真不应该写出这种话来。

葛罗斯特：　　给我看，给我看。

爱德蒙：　　我希望哥哥写这封信是有他的理由的，他不过要试试我的德性。

葛罗斯特：　　（读信）"这一种尊敬老年人的政策，使我们在年轻时候不能享受生命的欢乐；我们的财产不能由我们自己处分，等到年纪老了，这些财产对我们也失去了用处。我开始觉得老年人的专制，实在是一种荒谬愚蠢的束缚；他们没有权力压迫我们，是我们自己容忍他们的压迫。来跟我讨论讨论这一个问题吧。要是我们的父亲在我把他惊醒之前，一直好好睡着，你就可以永远享受他的一半的收入，并且将要为你的哥哥所喜爱。爱德伽。"——哼！阴谋！"要是我们的父亲在我把他惊醒之前，一直好好睡着，你就可以永远享受他的一半的收入。"我的儿子爱德伽！他会有这样的心思？他能写得出这样一封信吗？这封信是什么时候到你手里的？谁把它送给你的？

爱德蒙：　　它不是什么人送给我的，父亲；这正是他狡猾的地方；我看见它塞在我的房间的窗眼里。

葛罗斯特：　　你认识这笔迹是你哥哥的吗？

爱德蒙：　　父亲，要是这信里所写的都是很好的话，我敢发誓这是他的笔迹；可是那上面写的既然是这种话，我但愿不是他写的。

葛罗斯特：　　这是他的笔迹。

爱德蒙：　　笔迹确是他的，父亲；可是我希望这种话不是出于他的真心。

葛罗斯特：　　他以前有没有用这一类话试探过你？

business?

EDMUND.　Never, my lord. But I have heard him oft maintain it to be fit that, sons at perfect age, and fathers declining, the father should be as ward to the son, and the son manage his revenue.

EARL OF GLOSTER.　O villain, villain! His very opinion in the letter! Abhorred villain! Unnatural, detested, brutish villain! worse than brutish! Go, sirrah, seek him. I'll apprehend him. Abominable villain! Where is he?

EDMUND.　I do not well know, my lord. If it shall please you to suspend your indignation against my brother till you can derive from him better testimony of his intent, you should run a certain course; where, if you violently proceed against him, mistaking his purpose, it would make a great gap in your own honour and shake in pieces the heart of his obedience. I dare pawn down my life for him that he hath writ this to feel my affection to your honour, and to no other pretence of danger.

EARL OF GLOSTER.　Think you so?

EDMUND.　If your honour judge it meet, I will place you where you shall hear us confer of this and by an auricular assurance have your satisfaction, and that without any further delay than this very evening.

EARL OF GLOSTER.　He cannot be such a monster.

EDMUND.　Nor is not, sure.

EARL OF GLOSTER.　To his father, that so tenderly and entirely loves him. Heaven and earth! Edmund, seek him out; wind me into him, I pray you; frame the business after your own wisdom. I would unstate

爱德蒙：　　没有，父亲；可是我常常听见他说，儿子成年以后，父亲要是已经衰老，他应该受儿子的监护，把他的财产交给他的儿子掌管。

葛罗斯特：　　啊，混蛋！混蛋！正是他在这信里所表示的意思！可恶的混蛋！不孝的、没有心肝的畜生！禽兽不如的东西！去，把他找来；我要依法惩办他。可恶的混蛋！他在哪儿？

爱德蒙：　　我不大知道，父亲。照我的意思，你在没有得到可靠的证据，证明哥哥确有这种意思以前，最好暂时忍一忍您的怒气；因为要是您立刻就对他采取激烈的手段，万一事情出于误会，那不但大大妨害了您的尊严，而且他对于您的孝心，也要从此动摇了！我敢拿我的生命为他作保，他写这封信的用意，不过是试探试探我对您的孝心，并没有其他危险的目的。

葛罗斯特：　　你以为是这样的吗？

爱德蒙：　　您要是认为可以的话，让我把您安置在一个隐僻的地方，从那个地方您可以听到我们两人谈论这件事情，用您自己的耳朵得到一个真凭实据；事不宜迟，今天晚上就可以一试。

葛罗斯特：　　他不会是这样一个大逆不道的禽兽——

爱德蒙：　　他断不会是这样的人。

葛罗斯特：　　天地良心！我做父亲的从来没有亏待过他，他却这样对待我。爱德蒙，找他出来；探探他究竟居心何在；你尽管照你自己的意思随机应付。我愿意放弃我的地位和财产，把这一

myself to be in a due resolution.

EDMUND.   I will seek him, sir, presently; convey the business as I shall find means, and acquaint you withal.

EARL OF GLOSTER.   These late eclipses in the sun and moon portend no good to us. Though the wisdom of nature can reason it thus and thus, yet nature finds itself scourged by the sequent effects. Love cools, friendship falls off, brothers divide. In cities, mutinies; in countries, discord; in palaces, treason; and the bond cracked 'twixt son and father. This villain of mine comes under the prediction; there's son against father: the King falls from bias of nature; there's father against child. We have seen the best of our time. Machinations, hollowness, treachery, and all ruinous disorders follow us disquietly to our graves. Find out this villain, Edmund; it shall lose thee nothing; do it carefully. And the noble and true-hearted Kent banished! his offence, honesty! 'Tis strange
[*Exit.*]

EDMUND.   This is the excellent foppery of the world, that, when we are sick in fortune, often the surfeit of our own behaviour, we make guilty of our disasters the sun, the moon, and the stars; as if we were villains on necessity; fools by heavenly compulsion; knaves, thieves, and treachers by spherical pre-dominance; drunkards, liars, and adulterers by an enforced obedience of planetary influence; and all that we are evil in, by a divine thrusting on. An admirable evasion of whore-master man, to lay his goatish disposition to the charge of a star! My father compounded with my mother under the

件事情调查明白。

爱德蒙：　　父亲，我立刻就去找他，用最适当的方法探明这回事情，然后再来告诉您知道。

葛罗斯特：　　最近这一些日食月食果然不是好兆；虽然人们凭着天赋的智慧，可以对它们作种种合理的解释，可是接踵而来的天灾人祸，却不能否认是上天对人们所施的惩罚。亲爱的人互相疏远，朋友变为陌路，兄弟化成仇雠；城市里有暴动，国家发生内乱，宫廷之内潜藏着逆谋；父不父，子不子，纲常伦纪完全破灭。我这畜生也是上应天数；有他这样逆亲犯上的儿子，也就有像我们王上一样不慈不爱的父亲。我们最好的日子已经过去；现在只有一些阴谋、欺诈、叛逆、纷乱，追随在我们的背后，把我们赶下坟墓里去。爱德蒙，去把这畜生侦查个明白；那对你不会有什么妨害的；你只要自己留心一点就是了。——忠心的肯特又放逐了！他的罪名是正直！怪事，怪事！（下。）

爱德蒙：　　人们最爱用这一种糊涂思想来欺骗自己；往往当我们因为自己行为不慎而遭逢不幸的时候，我们就会把我们的灾祸归怨于日月星辰，好像我们做恶人也是命运注定，做傻瓜也是出于上天的旨意，做无赖、做盗贼、做叛徒，都是受到天体运行的影响，酗酒、造谣、奸淫，都有一颗什么星在那儿主持操纵，我们无论干什么罪恶的行为，全都是因为有一种超自然的力量在冥冥之中驱策着我们。明明自己跟人家通奸，却把他的好色的天性归咎到一颗星的身上，真是绝妙的推诿！我的父亲跟我的母亲在巨龙星的尾巴底下交媾，我又是在大熊星底下出世，

Dragon's Tail, and my nativity was under Ursa Major, so that it follows I am rough and lecherous. Fut! I should have been that I am, had the maidenliest star in the firmament twinkled on my bastardizing. Edgar – [*Enter Edgar.*] And pat! he comes, like the catastrophe of the old comedy. My cue is villainous melancholy, with a sigh like Tom o' Bedlam.O, these eclipses do portend these divisions! Fa, sol, la, mi.

EDGAR.　How now, brother Edmund? What serious contemplation are you in?

EDMUND.　I am thinking, brother, of a prediction I read this other day, what should follow these eclipses.

EDGAR.　Do you busy yourself with that?

EDMUND.　I promise you, the effects he writes of succeed unhappily: as of unnaturalness between the child and the parent; death, dearth, dissolutions of ancient amities; divisions in state, menaces and maledictions against king and nobles; needless diffidences, banishment of friends, dissipation of cohorts, nuptial breaches, and I know not what.

EDGAR.　How long have you been a sectary astronomical?

EDMUND.　Come, come! When saw you my father last?

EDGAR.　The night gone by.

EDMUND.　Spake you with him?

EDGAR.　Ay, two hours together.

EDMUND.　Parted you in good terms? Found you no displeasure in him by word or countenance.

EDGAR.　None at all.

所以我就是个粗暴而好色的家伙。嘿！即使当我的父母苟合成奸的时候，有一颗最贞洁的处女星在天空睒眼睛，我也绝不会换个样子的。爱德伽——（爱德伽上。）一说起他，他就来了，正像旧式喜剧里的大团圆一样；我现在必须装出一副忧愁煞人的样子，像疯子一般长吁短叹。唉！这些日食月食果然预兆着人世的纷争！法——索——拉——咪。

爱德伽：　啊，爱德蒙兄弟！你在沉思些什么？

爱德蒙：　哥哥，我正在想起前天读到的一篇预言，说是在这些日食月食之后，将要发生些什么事情。

爱德伽：　你让这些东西烦扰你的精神吗？

爱德蒙：　告诉你吧，他所预言的事情，果然不幸被他说中了；什么父子的乖离、死亡、饥荒、友谊的毁灭、国家的分裂、对于国王和贵族的恫吓和诅咒、无谓的猜疑、朋友的放逐、军队的瓦解、婚姻的破坏，还有许许多多我所不知道的事情。

爱德伽：　你什么时候相信起星象之学来？

爱德蒙：　来，来；你最近一次看见父亲在什么时候？

爱德伽：　昨天晚上。

爱德蒙：　你跟他说过话没有？

爱德伽：　嗯，我们谈了两个钟头。

爱德蒙：　你们分别的时候，没有闹什么意见吗？你在他的辞色之间，不觉得他对你有点恼怒吗？

爱德伽：　一点没有。

EDMUND. Bethink yourself wherein you may have offended him; and at my entreaty forbear his presence until some little time hath qualified the heat of his displeasure, which at this instant so rageth in him that with the mischief of your person it would scarcely allay.

EDGAR. Some villain hath done me wrong.

EDMUND. That's my fear. I pray you have a continent forbearance till the speed of his rage goes slower; and, as I say, retire with me to my lodging, from whence I will fitly bring you to hear my lord speak. Pray ye, go! There's my key. If you do stir abroad, go armed.

EDGAR. Armed, brother?

EDMUND. Brother, I advise you to the best. Go armed. I am no honest man if there be any good meaning toward you. I have told you what I have seen and heard; but faintly, nothing like the image and horror of it. Pray you, away!

EDGAR. Shall I hear from you anon?

EDMUND. I do serve you in this business.

[Exit Edgar.]

A credulous father! and a brother noble,

Whose nature is so far from doing harms

That he suspects none; on whose foolish honesty

My practices ride easy! I see the business.

Let me, if not by birth, have lands by wit;

All with me's meet that I can fashion fit. [*Exit.*]

爱德蒙： 想想看你在什么地方得罪了他；听我的劝告，暂时避开一下，等他的怒气平息下来再说，现在他正在大发雷霆，恨不得一口咬下你的肉来呢。

爱德伽： 一定有哪一个坏东西在搬弄是非。

爱德蒙： 我也怕有什么人在暗中离间。请你千万忍耐忍耐，不要碰在他的火性上；现在你还是跟我到我的地方去，我可以想法让你躲起来听听他老人家怎么说。请你去吧；这是我的钥匙。你要是在外面走动的话，最好身边带些武器。

爱德伽： 带些武器，弟弟！

爱德蒙： 哥哥，我这样劝告你都是为了你的好处；带些武器在身边吧；要是没有人在暗算你，就算我不是个好人。我已经把我所看到、听到的事情都告诉你了；可还只是轻描淡写，实际的情形，却比我的话更要严重可怕得多哩。请你赶快去吧。

爱德伽： 我不久就可以听到你的消息吗？

爱德蒙： 我在这一件事情上总是竭力帮你的忙就是了。（爱德伽下。）一个轻信的父亲，一个忠厚的哥哥，他自己从不会算计别人，所以也不疑心别人算计他；对付他们这样老实的傻瓜，我的奸计是绰绰有余的。该怎么下手，我已经想好了。既然凭我的身份，产业到不了我的手，那就只好用我的智谋；不管什么手段只要使得上，对我说来，就是正当。（下。）

ACT I   SCENE III

The Duke of Albany's Palace.
[*Enter Goneril and her Steward Oswald.*]

GONERIL.   Did my father strike my gentleman for chiding of his
  fool?

OSWALD.   Ay, madam.

GONERIL.   By day and night, he wrongs me! Every hour

  He flashes into one gross crime or other

  That sets us all at odds. I'll not endure it.

  His knights grow riotous, and himself upbraids us

  On every trifle. When he returns from hunting,

  I will not speak with him. Say I am sick.

  If you come slack of former services,

  You shall do well; the fault of it I'll answer.

  [*Horns within.*]

OSWALD.   He's coming, madam; I hear him

GONERIL.   Put on what weary negligence you please,

  You and your fellows. Ied have it come to question.

  If he distaste it, let him to our sister,

  Whose mind and mine I know in that are one,

  Not to be overruled. Idle old man,

第一幕　第三场

奥本尼公爵府中一室。

（高纳里尔及其管家奥斯华德上。）

高纳里尔：　我的父亲因为我的侍卫骂了他的弄人，所以动手打他
　　　　　吗？

奥斯华德：　是，夫人。

高纳里尔：　他一天到晚欺侮我；每一点钟他都要借端寻事，把我
　　　　　们这儿吵得鸡犬不宁。我不能再忍受下去了。他的骑士们一天
　　　　　一天横行不法起来，他自己又在每一件小事上都要责骂我们。
　　　　　等他打猎回来的时候，我不高兴见他说话；你就对他说我病了。
　　　　　你也不必像从前那样殷勤侍候他；他要是见怪，都在我身上。

　　　　　（内号角声。）

奥斯华德：　他来了，夫人；我听见他的声音。

高纳里尔：　你跟你手下的人尽管对他装出一副不理不睬的态度；
　　　　　我要看看他有些什么话说。要是他恼了，那么让他到我妹妹那
　　　　　儿去吧，我知道我的妹妹的心思，她也跟我一样不能受人压制
　　　　　的。这老废物已经放弃了他的权力，还想管这个管那个！凭着
　　　　　我的生命发誓，年老的傻瓜正像小孩子一样，一味的姑息会纵

That still would manage those authorities

That he hath given away! Now, by my life,

Old fools are babes again, and must be used

With checks as flatteries, when they are seen abused.

Remember what I have said.

OSWALD.   Very well, madam.

GONERIL.   And let his knights have colder looks among you.

What grows of it, no matter. Advise your fellows so.

I would breed from hence occasions, and I shall,

That I may speak. I'll write straight to my sister

To hold my very course. Prepare for dinner.

[*Exeunt.*]

容坏了他的脾气，不对他凶一点是不行的，记住我的话。

奥斯华德：　是，夫人。

高纳里尔：　让他的骑士们也受到你们的冷眼；无论发生什么事情，你们都不用管；你去这样通知你手下的人吧。我要造成一些借口，和他当面说个明白。我还要立刻写信给我的妹妹，叫她采取一致的行动。吩咐他们备饭。（各下。）

ACT I   SCENE IV

The Duke of Albany's Palace.
[*Enter Kent, disguised.*]

EARL OF KENT.   If but as well I other accents borrow,
That can my speech defuse, my good intent
May carry through itself to that full issue
For which I razed my likeness. Now, banished Kent,
If thou canst serve where thou dost stand condemned,
So may it come, thy master, whom thou lov'st,
Shall find thee full of labours.

[*Horns within.*]
[*Enter Lear, Knights, and Attendants.*]

KING LEAR.   Let me not stay a jot for dinner; go get it ready.
[*Exit an Attendant.*]
How now? What art thou?
EARL OF KENT.   A man, sir.
KING LEAR.   What dost thou profess? What wouldst thou with us?
EARL OF KENT.   I do profess to be no less than I seem, to serve him
truly that will put me in trust, to love him that is honest, to converse

第一幕 第四场

奥本尼公爵府中厅堂。
（肯特化装上。）

肯特：　我已经完全隐去我的本来面目，要是我能够把我的语音也
　　　完全改变过来，那么我的一片苦心，也许可以达到目的。被放
　　　逐的肯特啊，要是你顶着一身罪名，还依然能够尽你的忠心，
　　　那么总有一天，对你所爱戴的主人会大有用处的。

（内号角声。）
（李尔、众骑士及侍从等上。）

李尔：　我一刻也不能等待，快去叫他们拿出饭来。（一侍从下。）
　　　啊！你是什么？

肯特：　我是一个人，大爷。
李尔：　你是干什么的？你来见我有什么事？
肯特：　您瞧我像干什么的，我就是干什么的；谁要是信任我，我
　　　愿意尽忠服侍他；谁要是居心正直，我愿意爱他；谁要是聪明

with him that is wise and says little, to fear judgment, to fight when I cannot choose, and to eat no fish.

KING LEAR.   What are thou?

EARL OF KENT.   A very honest-hearted fellow, and as poor as the king.

KING LEAR.   If thou be as poor for a subject as he is for a king, thou art poor enough. What wouldst thou?

EARL OF KENT.   Service.

KING LEAR.   Who wouldst thou serve?

EARL OF KENT.   You.

KING LEAR.   Dost thou know me,fellow?

EARL OF KENT.   No, sir; but you have that in your countenance which I would fain call master.

KING LEAR.   What's that?

EARL OF KENT.   Authotity.

KING LEAR.   What services canst thou do?

EARL OF KENT.   I can keep honest counsel, ride, run, mar a curious tale in telling it and deliver a plain message bluntly. That which ordinary men are fit for, I am qualified in, and the best of me is diligence.

KING LEAR.   How old art thou?

EARL OF KENT.   Not so young, sir, to love a woman for singing, nor so old to dote on her for anything. I have years on my back forty-eight.

KING LEAR.   Follow me; thou shalt serve me. If I like thee no worse after dinner, I will not part from thee yet. Dinner, ho, dinner!

而不爱多说话，我愿意跟他来往；我害怕法官；逼不得已的时候，我也会跟人家打架；我不吃鱼[1]。

李尔：　你究竟是什么人？

肯特：　一个心肠非常正直的汉子，而且像国王一样穷。

李尔：　要是你这做臣民的，也像那个做国王的一样穷，那么你也可以算得真穷了。你要什么？

肯特：　就要讨一个差使。

李尔：　你想替谁做事？

肯特：　替您。

李尔：　你认识我吗？

肯特：　不，大爷；可是在您的神气之间，有一种什么力量，使我愿意叫您做我的主人。

李尔：　是什么力量？

肯特：　一种天生的威严。

李尔：　你会做些什么事？

肯特：　我会保守秘密，我会骑马，我会跑路，我会把一个复杂的故事讲得索然无味，我会老老实实传一个简单的口信；凡是普通人能够做的事情，我都可以做，我的最大的好处是勤劳。

李尔：　你年纪多大了？

肯特：　大爷，说我年轻，我也不算年轻，我不会为了一个女人会唱几句歌而害相思；说我年老，我也不算年老，我不会糊里糊涂地溺爱一个女人；我已经活过四十八个年头了。

李尔：　跟着我吧；你可以替我做事。要是我在吃过晚饭以后，还

[1] 意指肯特不是天主教徒，天主教徒每逢星期五按例吃鱼。

Where's my knave? my fool? Go you and call my fool hither. [*Exit an attendant. Enter Oswald the Steward.*] You, you, sirrah, where's my daughter?

OSWALD.　So please you –

[*Exit.*]

KING LEAR.　What says the fellow there? Call the clotpoll back. [*Exit a Knight.*] Where's my fool, ho? I think the world's asleep. [*Enter Knight.*] How now? Where's that mongrel?

KNIGHT.　He says, my lord, your daughter is not well.

KING LEAR.　Why came not the slave back to me when I called him?

KNIGHT.　Sir, he answered me in the roundest manner, he would not.

KING LEAR.　He would not?

KNIGHT.　My lord, I know not what the matter is; but to my judgment your Highness is not entertained with that ceremonious affection as you were wont. There's a great abatement of kindness appears as well in the general dependants as in the Duke himself also and your daughter.

KING LEAR.　Ha! say'st thou so?

KNIGHT.　I beseech you pardon me, my lord, if I be mistaken; for my duty cannot be silent when I think your Highness wronged.

KING LEAR.　Thou but rememberest me of mine own conception. I have perceived a most faint neglect of late, which I have rather blamed as mine own jealous curiosity than as a very pretence and purpose of unkindness. I will look further into't. But where's my fool? I have not seen him this two days.

是这样欢喜你，那么我还不会就把你撵走。喂！饭呢？拿饭来！我的孩子呢？我的傻瓜呢？你去叫我的傻瓜来。（一侍从下。）（奥斯华德上。）喂，喂，我的女儿呢？

奥斯华德： 对不起——（下。）

李尔： 这家伙怎么说？叫那蠢东西回来。（一骑士下。）喂，我的傻瓜呢？全都睡着了吗？（骑士重上。）怎么！那狗头呢？

骑士： 陛下，他说公主有病。

李尔： 我叫他回来，那奴才为什么不回来？

骑士： 陛下，他非常放肆，回答我说他不高兴回来。

李尔： 他不高兴回来！

骑士： 陛下，我也不知道为了什么缘故，可是照我看起来，他们对待您的礼貌，已经不像往日那样殷勤了；不但一般下人从仆，就是公爵和公主也对您冷淡得多了。

李尔： 嘿！你这样说吗？

骑士： 陛下，要是我说错了话，请您原谅我；可是当我觉得您受人欺侮的时候，责任所在，我不能闭口不言。

李尔： 你不过向我提起一件我自己已经感觉到的事；我近来也觉得他们对我的态度有点儿冷淡，可是我总以为那是我自己多心，不愿断定是他们有意怠慢。我还要仔细观察观察他们的举止。可是我的傻瓜呢？我这两天没有看见他。

KNIGHT.　Since my young lady's going into France, sir, the fool hath much pined away.

KING LEAR.　No more of that; I have noted it well.

Go you and tell my daughter I would speak with her.

[*Exit an Attendant.*]

Go you, call hither my fool.

[*Exit an Attendant.*]

[*Enter Oswald the Steward.*]

KING LEAR.　O, you, sir, you! Come you hither, sir. Who am I, sir?

OSWALD.　My lady's father.

KING LEAR.　My lady's father? My lord's knave! You whoreson dog! You slave! you cur!

OSWALD.　I am none of these, my lord; I beseech your pardon.

KING LEAR.　Do you bandy looks with me, you rascal?

[*Strikes him.*]

OSWALD.　I'll not be strucken, my lord.

EARL OF KENT.　Nor tripped neither, you base football player?

[*Trips up his heels.*]

KING LEAR.　I thank thee, fellow. Thou serv'st me, and I'll love thee.

EARL OF KENT.　Come, sir, arise, away! I'll teach you differences. Away, away! If you will measure your lubber's length again, tarry; but away! Go to! Have you wisdom? So.

[*Pushes him out.*]

骑士：　陛下，自从小公主到法国去了以后，这傻瓜老是郁郁不乐。

李尔：　别再提那句话了；我也注意到他这种情形。——你去对我的女儿说，我要跟她说话。（一侍从下。）你去叫我的傻瓜来。（另一侍从下。）

（奥斯华德重上。）

李尔：　啊！你，大爷，你过来，大爷。你不知道我是什么人吗，大爷？

奥斯华德：　我们夫人的父亲。

李尔：　"我们夫人的父亲"！我们大爷的奴才！好大胆的狗！你这奴才！你这狗东西！

奥斯华德：　对不起，我不是狗。

李尔：　你敢跟我当面顶嘴瞪眼吗，你这混蛋？（打奥斯华德。）

奥斯华德：　您不能打我。

肯特：　我也不能踢你吗，你这踢皮球的下贱东西？（自后踢奥斯华德倒地。）

李尔：　谢谢你，好家伙；你帮了我，我喜欢你。

肯特：　来，朋友，站起来，给我滚吧！我要教训教训你，让你知道尊卑上下的分别。去！去！你还想用你蠢笨的身体在地上打滚，丈量土地吗？滚！你难道不懂得厉害吗？去。（将奥斯华德推出。）

KING LEAR.   Now, my friendly knave, I thank thee. There's earnest of thy service.

[*Gives money.*]

[*Enter Fool.*]

FOOL.   Let me hire him too. Here's my coxcomb.

[*Offers Kent his cap.*]

KING LEAR.   How now, my pretty knave? How dost thou?

FOOL.   Sirrah, you were best take my coxcomb.

EARL OF KENT.   Why, fool?

FOOL.   Why? For taking one's part that's out of favour. Nay, an thou canst not smile as the wind sits, thou'lt catch cold shortly. There, take my coxcomb! Why, this fellow hath banished two on's daughters, and did the third a blessing against his will. If thou follow him, thou must needs wear my coxcomb. – How now, nuncle? Would I had two coxcombs and two daughters!

KING LEAR.   Why, my boy?

FOOL.   If I gave them all my living, I'ld keep my coxcombs myself. There's mine! Beg another of thy daughters.

KING LEAR.   Take heed, sirrah – the whip.

FOOL.   Truth's a dog must to kennel; he must be whipped out, when Lady the brach may stand by th' fire and stink.

KING LEAR.   A pestilent gall to me!

FOOL.   Sirrah, I'll teach thee a speech.

李尔：　　我的好小子，谢谢你；这是你替我做事的定钱。（以钱给
　　　　　肯特。）

（弄人上。）

弄人：　　让我也把他雇下来；这儿是我的鸡头帽。（脱帽授肯特。）

李尔：　　啊，我的乖乖！你好？
弄人：　　喂，你还是戴了我的鸡头帽吧。
肯特：　　傻瓜，为什么？
弄人：　　为什么？因为你帮了一个失势的人。要是你不会看准风向
　　　　　把你的笑脸迎上去，你就会吞下一口冷气的。来，把我的鸡头
　　　　　帽拿去。嘿，这家伙撵走了两个女儿，他的第三个女儿倒很受
　　　　　他的好处，虽然也不是出于他的本意；要是你跟了他，你必须
　　　　　戴上我的鸡头帽。啊，老伯伯！但愿我有两顶鸡头帽，再有两
　　　　　个女儿！
李尔：　　为什么，我的孩子？
弄人：　　要是我把我的家私一起给了她们，我自己还可以存下两顶
　　　　　鸡头帽。我这儿有一顶；再去向你的女儿们讨一顶戴戴吧。
李尔：　　嘿，你留心着鞭子。
弄人：　　真理是一条贱狗，它只好躲在狗洞里；当猎狗太太站在火
　　　　　边撒尿的时候，它必须一顿鞭子被人赶出去。
李尔：　　简直是揭我的疮疤！
弄人：　　（向肯特）喂，让我教你一段话。

KING LEAR.   Do.

FOOL.   Mark it, nuncle.

> Have more than thou showest,
>
> Speak less than thou knowest,
>
> Lend less than thou owest,
>
> Ride more than thou goest,
>
> Learn more than thou trowest,
>
> Set less than thou throwest;
>
> Leave thy drink and thy whore,
>
> And keep in-a-door,
>
> And thou shalt have more
>
> Than two tens to a score.

EARL OF KENT.   This is nothing, fool.

FOOL.   Then 'tis like the breath of an unfeed lawyer – you gave me nothing for't. Can you make no use of nothing, nuncle?

KING LEAR.   Why, no, boy. Nothing can be made out of nothing.

FOOL.   [*To Kent.*] Prithee tell him, so much the rent of his land comes to. He will not believe a fool.

KING LEAR.   A bitter fool!

FOOL.   Dost thou know the difference, my boy, between a bitter fool and a sweet fool?

KING LEAR.   No, lad; teach me.

FOOL.   That lord that counselled thee

> To give away thy land,
>
> Come place him here by me –
>
> Do thou for him stand.

李尔：　你说吧。

弄人：　听着，老伯伯；——

多积财，少摆阔；

耳多听，话少说；

少放款，多借债；

走路不如骑马快；

三言之中信一语，

多掷骰子少下注；

莫饮酒，莫嫖妓；

待在家中把门闭；

会打算的占便宜，

不会打算叹口气。

肯特：　傻瓜，这些话一点意思也没有。

弄人：　那么正像拿不到讼费的律师一样，我的话都白说了。老伯伯，你不能从没有意思的中间，探求出一点意思来吗？

李尔：　啊，不，孩子；垃圾里是淘不出金子来的。

弄人：　（向肯特）请你告诉他，他有那么多的土地，也就成为一堆垃圾了；他不肯相信一个傻瓜嘴里的话。

李尔：　好尖酸的傻瓜！

弄人：　我的孩子，你知道傻瓜是有酸有甜的吗？

李尔：　不，孩子；告诉我。

弄人：　听了他人话，

土地全丧失；

我傻你更傻，

两傻相并立：

The sweet and bitter fool

Will presently appear;

The one in motley here,

The other found out there.

KING LEAR.　Dost thou call me fool, boy?

FOOL.　All thy other titles thou hast given away; that thou wast born with.

EARL OF KENT.　This is not altogether fool, my lord.

FOOL.　No, faith; lords and great men will not let me. If I had a monopoly out, they would have part on't. And ladies too, they will not let me have all the fool to myself; they'll be snatching. Give me an egg, nuncle, and I'll give thee two crowns.

KING LEAR.　What two crowns shall they be?

FOOL.　Why, after I have cut the egg i' th' middle and eat up the meat, the two crowns of the egg. When thou clovest thy crown i' th' middle and gav'st away both parts, thou bor'st thine ass on thy back o'er the dirt. Thou hadst little wit in thy bald crown when thou gav'st thy golden one away. If I speak like myself in this, let him be whipped that first finds it so.

[*Sings.*]

Fools had ne'er less grace in a year,

For wise men are grown foppish;

They know not how their wits to wear,

Their manners are so apish.

KING LEAR.　When were you wont to be so full of songs, sirrah?

一个傻瓜甜，

一个傻瓜酸；

一个穿花衣，

一个戴王冠。

李尔：　你叫我傻瓜吗，孩子？

弄人：　你把你所有的尊号都送了别人；只有这一个名字是你娘胎里带来的。

肯特：　陛下，他倒不全然是个傻瓜哩。

弄人：　不，那些老爷大人们都不肯答应我的；要是我取得了傻瓜的专利权，他们一定要来夺我一份去，就是太太小姐们也不会放过我的；他们不肯让我一个人做傻瓜。老伯伯，给我一个蛋，我给你两顶冠。

李尔：　两顶什么冠？

弄人：　我把蛋从中间切开，吃完了蛋黄、蛋白，就用蛋壳给你做两顶冠。你想你自己好端端有了一顶王冠，却把它从中间剖成两半，把两半全都送给人家，这不是背了驴子过泥潭吗？你这光秃秃的头顶连里面也是光秃秃的没有一点脑子，所以才会把一顶金冠送了人。我说了我要说的话，谁说这种话是傻话，让他挨一顿鞭子。——

（唱。）

这年头傻瓜供过于求，

聪明人个个变了糊涂，

顶着个没有思想的头，

只会跟着人依样葫芦。

李尔：　你几时学会了这许多歌儿？

FOOL.   I have used it, nuncle, ever since thou madest thy daughters thy mother; for when thou gavest them the rod, and put'st down thine own breeches,

[*Sings.*]

Then they for sudden joy did weep,

And I for sorrow sung,

That such a king should play bo-peep

And go the fools among.

Prithee, nuncle, keep a schoolmaster that can teach thy fool to lie. I would fain learn to lie.

KING LEAR.   An you lie, sirrah, we'll have you whipped.

FOOL.   I Marvel what kin thou and thy daughters are. They'll have me whipped for speaking true; thou'lt have me whipped for lying; and sometimes I am whipped for holding my peace. I had rather be any kind o' thing than a fool! And yet I would not be thee, nuncle. Thou hast pared thy wit o' both sides and left nothing i' th' middle. Here comes one o' the parings.

[*Enter Goneril.*]

KING LEAR.   How now, daughter? What makes that frontlet on? Methinks you are too much o' late i' th' frown.

FOOL.   Thou wast a pretty fellow when thou hadst no need to care for her frowning.

Now thou art an O without a figure. I am better than thou art now: I am a fool, thou art nothing.

弄人：　老伯伯，自从你把你的女儿当做了你的母亲以后，我就常常唱起歌儿来了；因为当你把棒儿给了她们，拉下你自己的裤子的时候，——

（唱。）

> 她们高兴得眼泪盈眶，
> 我只好唱歌自遣哀愁，
> 可怜你堂堂一国之王，
> 却跟傻瓜们做伴嬉游。

老伯伯，你去请一位先生来，教教你的傻瓜怎样说谎吧；我很想学学说谎。

李尔：　要是你说了谎，小子，我就用鞭子抽你。

弄人：　我不知道你跟你的女儿们究竟是什么亲戚：她们因为我说了真话，要用鞭子抽我，你因为我说谎，又要用鞭子抽我；有时候我话也不说，你们也要用鞭子抽我。我宁可做一个无论什么东西，也不要做个傻瓜；可是我宁可做个傻瓜，也不愿意做你，老伯伯；你把你的聪明从两边削掉了，削得中间不剩一点东西。瞧，那削下的　一块来了。

（高纳里尔上。）

李尔：　啊，女儿！为什么你的脸上罩满了怒气？我看你近来老是皱着眉头。

弄人：　从前你用不着看她的脸，随她皱不皱眉头都不与你相干，那时候你也算得了一个好汉子；可是现在你却变成一个孤零零的圆圈圈儿了。你还比不上我；我是个傻瓜，你简直不是个东西。（向高纳里尔）好，好，我闭嘴就是啦；虽然你没有说话，

[*To Goneril.*]

Yes, forsooth, I will hold my tongue. So your face bids me, though you say nothing.

Mum, mum!

He that keeps nor crust nor crum,

Weary of all, shall want some. –

That's a shelled peascod.

[*Points at Lear.*]

GONERIL. Not only, sir, this your all-licensed fool,

But other of your insolent retinue

Do hourly carp and quarrel, breaking forth

In rank and not-to-be-endured riots. Sir,

I had thought, by making this well known unto you,

To have found a safe redress, but now grow fearful,

By what yourself, too, late have spoke and done,

That you protect this course, and put it on

By your allowance; which if you should, the fault

Would not scape censure, nor the redresses sleep,

Which, in the tender of a wholesome weal,

Might in their working do you that offence

Which else were shame, that then necessity

Must call discreet proceeding.

FOOL.   For you know, nuncle,

The hedge-sparrow fed the cuckoo so long

That it had it head bit off by it young.

So out went the candle, and we were left darkling.

我从你的脸色知道你的意思。

闭嘴，闭嘴；
你不知道积谷防饥，
活该啃不到面包皮。
他是一个剥空了的豌豆荚。（指李尔。）

高纳里尔：　父亲，您这一个肆无忌惮的傻瓜不用说了，还有您那
　　　　　些蛮横的卫士，也都在时时刻刻寻事骂人，种种不法的暴行，
　　　　　实在叫人忍无可忍。父亲，我本来还以为要是让您知道了这种
　　　　　情形，您一定会戒饬他们的行动；可是照您最近所说的话和所
　　　　　做的事看来，我不能不疑心您有意纵容他们，他们才会这样有
　　　　　恃无恐。要是果然出于您的授意，为了维持法纪的尊严，我们
　　　　　也不能默尔而息，不采取断然的处置，虽然也许在您的脸上不
　　　　　大好看；本来，这是说不过去的，可是眼前这样的步骤，在事
　　　　　实上却是必要的。

弄人：　你看，老伯伯——
　　　　那篱雀养大了杜鹃鸟，
　　　　自己的头也给它吃掉。
　　　　蜡烛熄了，我们眼前只有一片黑暗。

KING LEAR.　Are you our daughter?

GONERIL.　Come, sir,

　　I would you would make use of that good wisdom

　　Whereof I know you are fraught, and put away

　　These dispositions that of late transform you

　　From what you rightly are.

FOOL.　May not an ass know when the cart draws the horse? Whoop,

　　Jug, I love thee!

KING LEAR.　Does any here know me? This is not Lear.

　　Does Lear walk thus? speak thus? Where are his eyes?

　　Either his notion weakens, his discernings

　　Are lethargied – Ha! waking? 'Tis not so!

　　Who is it that can tell me who I am?

FOOL.　Lear's shadow.

KING LEAR.　I would learn that; for, by the marks of sovereignty,

　　Knowledge, and reason, I should be false persuaded

　　I had daughters.

FOOL.　Which they will make an obedient father.

KING LEAR.　Your name, fair gentlewoman?

GONERIL.　This admiration, sir, is much o' th' savour

　　Of other your new pranks. I do beseech you

　　To understand my purposes aright.

　　As you are old and reverend, you should be wise.

　　Here do you keep a hundred knights and squires;

　　Men so disordered, so debauched, and bold

　　That this our court, infected with their manners,

李尔：　你是我的女儿吗？

高纳里尔：　算了吧，老人家，您不是一个不懂道理的人，我希望
　　您想明白一些；近来您动不动就动气，实在太有失一个做长辈
　　的体统啦。

弄人：　马儿颠倒过来给车子拖着走，就是一头蠢驴不也看得清楚
　　吗？"呼，玖格！我爱你。"

李尔：　这儿有谁认识我吗？这不是李尔。是李尔在走路吗？在说
　　话吗？他的眼睛呢？他的知觉迷乱了吗？他的神志麻木了吗？
　　嘿！他醒着吗？没有的事。谁能够告诉我我是什么人？

弄人：　李尔的影子。

李尔：　我要弄明白我是谁；因为我的君权、知识和理智都在哄我，
　　要我相信我是个有女儿的人。

弄人：　那些女儿们是会叫你做一个孝顺的父亲的。

李尔：　太太，请教您的芳名？

高纳里尔：　父亲，您何必这样假痴假呆，近来您就爱开这么一类
　　的玩笑。您是一个有年纪的老人家，应该懂事一些。请您明白
　　我的意思；您在这儿养了一百个骑士，全是些胡闹放荡、胆大
　　妄为的家伙，我们好好的宫廷给他们骚扰得像一个喧嚣的客店；
　　他们成天吃、喝、玩女人，简直把这儿当做了酒馆妓院，哪里
　　还是一座庄严的御邸。这一种可耻的现象，必须立刻设法纠正；
　　所以请您依了我的要求，酌量减少您的扈从的人数，只留下一

Shows like a riotous inn. Epicurism and lust

Make it more like a tavern or a brothel

Than a graced palace. The shame itself doth speak

For instant remedy. Be then desired

By her that else will take the thing she begs

A little to disquantity your train,

And the remainder that shall still depend

To be such men as may besort your age,

Which know themselves, and you.

KING LEAR.   Darkness and devils!

Saddle my horses! Call my train together!

Degenerate bastard, I'll not trouble thee;

Yet have I left a daughter.

GONERIL.   You strike my people, and your disordered rabble

Make servants of their betters.

[*Enter Albany.*]

KING LEAR.   Woe that too late repents! – [*To Albany.*] O, sir, are you
come?

Is it your will? Speak, sir! – Prepare my horses.

Ingratitude, thou marble-hearted fiend,

More hideous when thou show'st thee in a child

Than the sea-monster!

DUKE OF ALBANY.   Pray, sir, be patient.

KING LEAR.   [*To Goneril.*] Detested kite, thou liest!

My train are men of choice and rarest parts,

些适合于您的年龄、知道您的地位、也明白他们自己身份的人跟随您；要是您不答应，那么我没有法子，只好勉强执行了。

李尔：　地狱里的魔鬼！备起我的马来；召集我的侍从。没有良心的贱人！我不要麻烦你；我还有一个女儿哩。

高纳里尔：　你打我的用人，你那一班捣乱的流氓也不想想自己是什么东西，胆敢把他们上面的人像奴仆一样呼来叱去。

（奥本尼上。）

李尔：　唉！现在懊悔也来不及了。（向奥本尼）啊！你也来了吗？这是不是你的意思？你说。——替我备马。丑恶的海怪也比不上忘恩的儿女那样可怕。

奥本尼：　陛下，请您不要生气。
李尔：　（向高纳里尔）枭獍不如的东西！你说谎！我的卫士都是最有品行的人，他们懂得一切的礼仪，他们的一举一动，都不

That all particulars of duty know

And in the most exact regard support

The worships of their name. – O most small fault,

How ugly didst thou in Cordelia show!

Which, like an engine, wrenched my frame of nature

From the fixed place; drew from my heart all love

And added to the gall. O Lear, Lear, Lear!

Beat at this gate that let thy folly in

[*Strikes his head.*]

And thy dear judgment out! Go, go, my people.

DUKE OF ALBANY.　My lord, I am guiltless, as I am ignorant

Of what hath moved you.

KING LEAR.　It may be so, my lord.

Hear, Nature, hear! dear goddess, hear!

Suspend thy purpose, if thou didst intend

To make this creature fruitful.

Into her womb convey sterility;

Dry up in her the organs of increase;

And from her derogate body never spring

A babe to honour her! If she must teem,

Create her child of spleen, that it may live

And be athwart disnatured torment to her.

Let it stamp wrinkles in her brow of youth,

With cadent tears fret channels in her cheeks,

Turn all her mother's pains and benefits

To laughter and contempt, that she may feel

愧骑士之名。啊！考狄利娅不过犯了一点小小的错误，怎么在我的眼睛里却会变得这样丑恶！它像一座酷虐的刑具，扭曲了我的天性，抽干了我心里的慈爱，把苦味的怨恨灌了进去。啊，李尔！李尔！李尔！对准这一扇装进你的愚蠢、放出你的智慧的门，着力痛打吧！（自击其头。）去，去，我的人。

奥本尼：　陛下，我没有得罪您，我也不知道您为什么生气。

李尔：　也许不是你的错，公爵。——听着，造化的女神，听我的吁诉！要是你想使这畜生生男育女，请你改变你的意旨吧！取消她的生殖的能力，干涸她的产育的器官，让她的下贱的肉体里永远生不出一个子女来抬高她的身价！要是她必须生产，请你让她生下一个忤逆狂悖的孩子，使她终身受苦！让她年轻的额角上很早就刻了皱纹；眼泪流下她的面颊，磨成一道道的沟渠；她的鞠育的辛劳，只换到一声冷笑和一个白眼；让她也感觉到一个负心的孩子，比毒蛇的牙齿还要多么使人痛入骨髓！去，去！（下。）

How sharper than a serpent's tooth it is

To have a thankless child! Away, away!

[*Exit.*]

DUKE OF ALBANY.   Now, gods that we adore, whereof comes this?

GONERIL.   Never afflict yourself to know the cause;

But let his disposition have that scope

That dotage gives it.

[*Enter Lear.*]

KING LEAR.   What, fifty of my followers at a clap?

Within a fortnight?

DUKE OF ALBANY.   What's the matter, sir?

KING LEAR.   I'll tell thee.

[*To Goneril.*] Life and death! I am ashamed

That thou hast power to shake my manhood thus;

That these hot tears, which break from me perforce,

Should make thee worth them. Blasts and fogs upon thee!

Th' untented woundings of a father's curse

Pierce every sense about thee! – Old fond eyes,

Beweep this cause again, I'll pluck ye out,

And cast you, with the waters that you lo se,

To temper clay. Yea, is it come to this?

Let it be so. Yet have I left a daughter,

Who I am sure is kind and comfortable.

奥本尼：　　凭着我们敬奉的神明，告诉我这是怎么一回事？

高纳里尔：　　你不用知道为了什么原因；他老糊涂了，让他去发他的火吧。

（李尔重上。）

李尔：　　什么！我在这儿不过住了半个月，就把我的卫士一下子裁撤了五十名吗？

奥本尼：　　什么事，陛下？

李尔：　　等一等告诉你。（向高纳里尔）吸血的魔鬼！我真惭愧，你有这本事叫我在你的面前失去了大丈夫的气概，让我的热泪为了一个下贱的婢子而滚滚流出。愿毒风吹着你，恶雾罩着你！愿一个父亲的诅咒刺透你的五官百窍，留下永远不能平复的疮痍！痴愚的老眼，要是你再为此而流泪，我要把你挖出来，丢在你所流的泪水里，和泥土拌在一起！哼！竟有这等事吗？好，我还有一个女儿，我相信她是孝顺我的；她听见你这样对待我，一定会用指爪抓破你的豺狼一样的脸。你以为我一辈子也不能恢复我的原来的威风了吗？好，你瞧着吧。（李尔、肯特及侍从等下。）

When she shall hear this of thee, with her nails

She'll flay thy wolvish visage. Thou shalt find

That I'll resume the shape which thou dost think

I have cast off for ever.

[*Exeunt.*]

GONERIL.   Do you mark that, my lord?

DUKE OF ALBANY.   I cannot be so partial, Goneril,

To the great love I bear you –

GONERIL.   Pray you, content. – What, Oswald, ho!

[*To the Fool.*] You, sir, more knave than fool, after your master!

FOOL.   Nuncle Lear, nuncle Lear, tarry! Take the fool with thee.

A fox when one has caught her,

And such a daughter,

Should sure to the slaughter,

If my cap would buy a halter.

So the fool follows after.

[*Exit.*]

GONERIL.   This man hath had good counsel! A hundred knights?

'Tis politic and safe to let him keep

At point a hundred knights; yes, that on every dream,

Each buzz, each fancy, each complaint, dislike,

He may enguard his dotage with their powers

And hold our lives in mercy. – Oswald, I say!

DUKE OF ALBANY.   Well, you may fear too far.

GONERIL.   Safer than trust too far.

高纳里尔：　你听见没有？

奥本尼：　高纳里尔，虽然我十分爱你，可是我不能这样偏心——

高纳里尔：　你不用管我。喂，奥斯华德！（向弄人）你这七分奸刁三分傻的东西，跟你的主人去吧。

弄人：　李尔老伯伯，李尔老伯伯！等一等，带傻瓜一块儿去。

　　捉狐狸，杀狐狸，

　　谁家女儿是狐狸？

　　可惜我这顶帽子，

　　换不到一条绳子；

　　追上去，你这傻子。（下。）

高纳里尔：　不知道是什么人替他出的好主意。一百个骑士！让他随身带着一百个全副武装的卫士，真是万全之计；只要他做了一个梦，听了一句谣言，转了一个念头，或者心里有什么不高兴不舒服，就可以任着性子，用他们的力量危害我们的生命。喂，奥斯华德！

奥本尼：　也许你太过虑了。

高纳里尔：　过虑总比大意好些。与其时时刻刻提心吊胆，害怕人

Let me still take away the harms I fear,

Not fear still to be taken. I know his heart.

What he hath uttered I have writ my sister.

If she sustain him and his hundred knights,

When I have showed th' unfitness –

[*Enter Oswald the Steward.*]

GONERIL.   How now, Oswald?

What, have you writ that letter to my sister?

OSWALD.   Yes, madam.

GONERIL.   Take you some company, and away to horse!

Inform her full of my particular fear,

And thereto add such reasons of your own

As may compact it more. Get you gone,

And hasten your return.

[*Exit Oswald.*]

No, no, my lord!

This milky gentleness and course of yours,

Though I condemn it not, yet, under pardon,

You are much more at task for want of wisdom

Than praised for harmful mildness.

DUKE OF ALBANY.   How far your eyes may pierce I cannot tell.

Striving to better, oft we mar what's well.

GONERIL.   Nay then –

DUKE OF ALBANY.   Well, well; th' event.

[*Exeunt.*]

家的暗算，宁可爽爽快快除去一切可能的威胁。我知道他的心理。他所说的话，我已经写信去告诉我的妹妹了；她要是不听我的劝告，仍旧容留他带着他的一百个骑士——

（奥斯华德重上。）

高纳里尔：　啊，奥斯华德！什么！我叫你写给我妹妹的信，你写好了没有？

奥斯华德：　写好了，夫人。

高纳里尔：　带几个人跟着你，赶快上马出发；把我所担心的情形明白告诉她，再加上一些你所想到的理由，让它格外动听一些。去吧，早点回来。（奥斯华德下。）不，不，我的爷，你做人太仁善厚道了，虽然我不怪你，可是恕我说一句话，只有人批评你糊涂，却没有什么人称赞你一声好。

奥本尼：　我不知道你的眼光能够看到多远；可是过分操切也会误事的。

高纳里尔：　咦，那么——

奥本尼：　好，好，但看结果如何。（同下。）

ACT I   SCENE V

Court before the Duke of Albany's Palace.

[*Enter Lear, Kent, and Fool.*]

KING LEAR.   Go you before to Gloster with these letters. Acquaint my daughter no further with anything you know than comes from her demand out of the letter. If your diligence be not speedy, I shall be there afore you.

EARL OF KENT.   I will not sleep, my lord, till I have delivered your letter.

[*Exit.*]

FOOL.   If a man's brains were in's heels, were't not in danger of kibes?

KING LEAR.   Ay, boy.

FOOL.   Then I prithee be merry. Thy wit shall ne'er go slip-shod.

KING LEAR.   Ha, ha, ha!

FOOL.   Shalt see thy other daughter will use thee kindly; for though she's as like this as a crab's like an apple, yet I can tell what I can tell.

KING LEAR.   What canst tell, boy?

FOOL.   She'll taste as like this as a crab does to a crab. Thou canst tell

第一幕　第五场

奥本尼公爵府外院。

（李尔、肯特及弄人上。）

李尔：　你带着这封信，先到葛罗斯特去。我的女儿看了我的信，倘然有什么话问你，你就照你所知道的回答她，此外可不要多说什么。要是你在路上偷懒耽搁时间，也许我会比你先到的。

肯特：　陛下，我在没有把您的信送到以前，绝不打一次盹。（下。）

弄人：　要是一个人的脑筋生在脚跟上，它会不会长起脓包来呢？

李尔：　嗯，不会的，孩子。

弄人：　那么你放心吧；反正你的脑筋不用穿了拖鞋走路。

李尔：　哈哈哈！

弄人：　你到了你那另外一个女儿的地方，就可以知道她会待你多么好；因为虽然她跟这一个就像野苹果跟家苹果一样相像，可是我可以告诉你我所知道的事情。

李尔：　你可以告诉我什么，孩子？

弄人：　你一尝到她的滋味，就会知道她跟这一个完全相同，正像

why one's nose stands i' th' middle on's face?

KING LEAR.　No.

FOOL.　Why, to keep one's eyes of either side's nose, that what a man cannot smell out, he may spy into.

KING LEAR.　I did her wrong.

FOOL.　Canst tell how an oyster makes his shell?

KING LEAR.　No.

FOOL.　Nor I neither; but I can tell why a snail has a house.

KING LEAR.　Why?

FOOL.　Why, to put's head in; not to give it away to his daughters, and leave his horns without a case.

KING LEAR.　I will forget my nature. So kind a father! – Be my horses ready?

FOOL.　Thy asses are gone about 'em. The reason why the seven stars are no more than seven is a pretty reason.

KING LEAR.　Because they are not eight?

FOOL.　Yes indeed. Thou wouldst make a good fool.

KING LEAR.　To tak't again perforce! Monster ingratitude!

FOOL.　If thou wert my fool, nuncle, I'ld have thee beaten for being old before thy time.

KING LEAR.　How's that?

FOOL.　Thou shouldst not have been old till thou hadst been wise.

KING LEAR.　O, let me not be mad, not mad, sweet heaven! Keep me in temper; I would not be mad!

[*Enter a Gentleman.*]

两只野苹果一般没有分别。你能够告诉我为什么一个人的鼻子生在脸中间吗？

李尔：　不能。

弄人：　因为中间放了鼻子，两旁就可以安放眼睛；鼻子嗅不出来的，眼睛可以看个仔细。

李尔：　我对不起她——

弄人：　你知道牡蛎怎样造它的壳吗？

李尔：　不知道。

弄人：　我也不知道；可是我知道蜗牛为什么背着一个屋子。

李尔：　为什么？

弄人：　因为可以把它的头放在里面；它不会把它的屋子送给它的女儿，害得它的角也没有地方安顿。

李尔：　我也顾不得什么天性之情了。我这做父亲的有什么地方亏待了她！我的马儿都已经预备好了吗？

弄人：　你的驴子们正在那儿给你预备呢。北斗七星为什么只有七颗星，其中有一个绝妙的理由。

李尔：　因为它们没有第八颗吗？

弄人：　正是，一点不错；你可以做一个很好的傻瓜。

李尔：　用武力夺回来！忘恩负义的畜生！

弄人：　假如你是我的傻瓜，老伯伯，我就要打你，因为你不到时候就老了。

李尔：　那是什么意思？

弄人：　你应该懂得些世故再老呀。

李尔：　啊！不要让我发疯！天哪，抑制住我的怒气，不要让我发疯！我不想发疯！

（侍臣上。）

KING LEAR.　　How now? Are the horses ready?

GENTLEMAN.　　Ready, my lord.

KING LEAR.　　Come, boy.

FOOL.　　She that's a maid now, and laughs at my departure,

　　　　Shall not be a maid long, unless things be cut shorter.

　　　　[*Exeunt.*]

李尔：　　怎么！马预备好了吗？

侍臣：　　预备好了，陛下。

李尔：　　来，孩子。

弄人：　　哪一个姑娘笑我走这一遭，

　　　　　她的贞操眼看就要保不牢。（同下。）

ACT II   SCENE I

A court within the Castle of the Earl of Gloster.
[*Enter Edmund and Curan, meeting.*]

EDMUND.   Save thee, Curan.

CURAN.   And you, sir. I have been with your father, and given him notice that the Duke of Cornwall and Regan his Duchess will be here with him this night.

EDMUND.   How comes that?

CURAN.   Nay, I know not. You have heard of the news abroad – I mean the whispered ones, for they are yet but ear-kissing arguments?

EDMUND.   Not I. Pray you, what are they?

CURAN.   Have you heard of no likely wars toward 'twixt the two Dukes of Cornwall and Albany?

EDMUND.   Not a word.

CURAN.   You may do, then, in time. Fare you well, sir.
   [*Exit.*]

EDMUND.   The Duke be hcre to-night? The better! best!
   This weaves itself perforce into my business.
   My father hath set guard to take my brother;

第二幕　第一场

葛罗斯特伯爵城堡庭院。

（爱德蒙及克伦自相对方向上。）

爱德蒙：　　您好，克伦？

克伦：　　您好，公子。我刚才见过令尊，通知他康华尔公爵跟他的
　　　　夫人里根公主今天晚上要到这儿来拜访他。

爱德蒙：　　他们怎么要到这儿来？

克伦：　　我也不知道。您有没有听见外边的消息？我的意思是说，
　　　　人们交头接耳，在暗中互相传说的那些消息。

爱德蒙：　　我没有听见；请教是些什么消息？

克伦：　　您没有听见说起康华尔公爵也许会跟奥本尼公爵开战吗？

爱德蒙：　　一点没有听见。

克伦：　　那么您也许慢慢会听到的。再会，公子。（下。）

爱德蒙：　　公爵今天晚上到这儿来！那也好！再好没有了！我正好
　　　　利用这个机会。我的父亲已经叫人四处把守，要捉我的哥哥；
　　　　我还有一件不大好办的事情，必须赶快动手做起来。这事情要

And I have one thing, of a queasy question,

Which I must act. Briefness and fortune, work!

Brother, a word! Descend! Brother, I say!

[*Enter Edgar.*]

EDMUND.   My father watches. O sir, fly this place!

Intelligence is given where you are hid.

You have now the good advantage of the night.

Have you not spoken 'gainst the Duke of Cornwall?

He's coming hither; now, i' th' night, i' th' haste,

And Regan with him. Have you nothing said

Upon his party 'gainst the Duke of Albany?

Advise yourself.

EDGAR.   I am sure on't, not a word.

EDMUND.   I hear my father coming. Pardon me!

In cunning I must draw my sword upon you.

Draw, seem to defend yourself; now quit you well. –

Yield! Come before my father. Light, ho, here!

Fly, brother. – Torches, torches! –So farewell.

[*Exit Edgar.*]

Some blood drawn on me would beget opinion

[*Stabs his arm.*]

Of my more fierce endeavour. I have seen drunkards

Do more than this in sport. – Father, father! –

Stop, stop! No help?

做得敏捷迅速，但愿命运帮助我！——哥哥，跟你说一句话；
下来，哥哥！

（爱德伽上。）

爱德蒙：　父亲在那儿守着你。啊，哥哥！离开这个地方吧；有人
　　　　已经告诉他你躲在什么所在；趁着现在天黑，你快逃吧。你有
　　　　没有说过什么反对康华尔公爵的话？他也就要到这儿来了，在
　　　　这样的夜里，急急忙忙的。里根也跟着他来；你有没有站在他
　　　　这一边，说过奥本尼公爵什么话吗？想一想看。

爱德伽：　我真的一句话也没有说过。
爱德蒙：　我听见父亲来了；原谅我；我必须假装对你动武的样子；
　　　　拔出剑来，就像你在防御你自己一般；好好地应付一下吧。（高
　　　　声）放下你的剑；见我的父亲去！喂，拿火来！这儿！——逃
　　　　吧，哥哥。（高声）火把！火把！——再会。（爱德伽下。）身上
　　　　沾几点血，可以使他相信我真的作过一番凶猛的争斗。（以剑刺
　　　　伤手臂。）我曾经看见有些醉汉为了开玩笑的缘故，往往不顾死
　　　　活地割破他自己的皮肉。（高声）父亲！父亲！住手！住手！没
　　　　有人来帮我吗？

[*Enter Gloster, and Servants with torches.*]

EARL OF GLOSTER.   Now, Edmund, where's the villain?

EDMUND.   Here stood he in the dark, his sharp sword out,

　　Mumbling of wicked charms, conjuring the moon

　　To stand 's auspicious mistress.

EARL OF GLOSTER.   But where is he?

EDMUND.   Look, sir, I bleed.

EARL OF GLOSTER.   Where is the villain, Edmund?

EDMUND.   Fled this way, sir. When by no means he could –

EARL OF GLOSTER.   Pursue him, ho! Go after.

　　[*Exeunt some Servants*].

　　By no means what?

EDMUND.   Persuade me to the murther of your lordship;

　　But that I told him the revenging gods

　　'Gainst parricides did all their thunders bend; Spoke with how

　　manifold and strong a bond

　　The child was bound to th' father – sir, in fine,

　　Seeing how loathly opposite I stood

　　To his unnatural purpose, in fell motion

　　With his prepared sword he charges home

　　My unprovided body, lanced mine arm;

　　But when he saw my best alarumed spirits,

　　Bold in the quarrel's right, roused to th' encounter,

　　Or whether gasted by the noise I made,

　　Full suddenly he fled.

（葛罗斯特率众仆持火炬上。）

葛罗斯特：　爱德蒙，那畜生呢？

爱德蒙：　他站在这儿黑暗之中，拔出他的锋利的剑，嘴里念念有词，见神见鬼地请月亮帮他的忙。

葛罗斯特：　可是他在什么地方？

爱德蒙：　瞧，父亲，我流着血呢。

葛罗斯特：　爱德蒙，那畜生呢？

爱德蒙：　往这边逃去了，父亲。他看见他没有法子——

葛罗斯特：　喂，你们追上去！（若干仆人下。）"没有法子"什么？

爱德蒙：　没有法子劝我跟他同谋把您杀死；我对他说，疾恶如仇的神明看见弑父的逆子，是要用天雷把他殛死的；我告诉他儿子对于父亲的关系是多么深切而不可摧毁；总而言之一句话，他看见我这样憎恶他的荒谬的图谋，他就恼羞成怒，拔出他的早就预备好的剑，气势汹汹地向我毫无防卫的身上挺了过来，把我的手臂刺破了；那时候我也发起怒来，自恃理直气壮，跟他奋力对抗，他倒胆怯起来，也许因为听见我喊叫的声音，就飞也似的逃走了。

EARL OF GLOSTER.   Let him fly far.

> Not in this land shall he remain uncaught;
>
> And found – dispatch. The noble Duke my master,
>
> My worthy arch and patron, comes to-night.
>
> By his authority I will proclaim it
>
> That he which find, him shall deserve our thanks,
>
> Bringing the murderous caitiff to the stake;
>
> He that conceals him, death.

EDMUND.   When I dissuaded him from his intent

> And found him pight to do it, with curst speech
>
> I threatened to discover him. He replied,
>
> Thou unpossessing bastard, dost thou think,
>
> If I would stand against thee, would the reposal
>
> Of any trust, virtue, or worth in thee
>
> Make thy words faithed? No. What I should deny
>
> As this I would; ay, though thou didst produce
>
> My very character, I'ld turn it all
>
> To thy suggestion, plot, and damned practice;
>
> And thou must make a dullard of the world,
>
> If they not thought the profits of my death
>
> Were very pregnant and potential spurs
>
> To make thee seek it.

EARL OF GLOSTER.   Strong and fast'ned villain!

> Would he deny his letter? I never got him.
>
> [*Tucket within.*]
>
> Hark, the Duke's trumpets! I know not why he comes.

葛罗斯特：　　让他逃得远远的吧；除非逃到国外去，我们总有捉到他的一天；看他给我们捉住了还活得成活不成。公爵殿下，我的高贵的恩主，今晚要到这儿来啦，我要请他发出一道命令，谁要是能够把这杀人的懦夫捉住，交给我们绑在木桩上烧死，我们将要重重酬谢他；谁要是把他藏匿起来，一经发觉，就要把他处死。

爱德蒙：　　当他不听我的劝告，决意实行他的企图的时候，我就严辞恫吓他，对他说我要宣布他的秘密；可是他却回答我说，"你这个没份儿继承遗产的私生子！你以为要是我们两人立在敌对的地位，人家会相信你的道德品质，因而相信你所说的话吗？哼！我可以绝口否认——我自然要否认，即使你拿出我亲手写下的笔迹，我还可以反咬你一口，说这全是你的阴谋恶计；人们不是傻瓜，他们当然会相信你因为觊觎我死后的利益，所以才会起这样的毒心，想要害我的命。"

葛罗斯特：　　好狠心的畜生！他赖得掉他的信吗？他不是我生出来的。（内喇叭奏花腔。）听！公爵的喇叭。我不知道他来有什么事。我要把所有的城门关起来，看这畜生逃到哪儿去；公爵必须答应我这一个要求；而且我还要把他的小像各处传送，让

All ports I'll bar; the villain shall not scape;

The Duke must grant me that. Besides, his picture

I will send far and near, that all the kingdom

May have due note of him, and of my land,

Loyal and natural boy, I'll work the means

To make thee capable.

[*Enter Cornwall, Regan, and Attendants.*]

DUKE OF CORNWALL.   How now, my noble friend?

Since I came hither

Which I can call but now I have heard strange news.

REGAN.   If it be true, all vengeance comes too short

Which can pursue th' offender. How dost, my lord?

EARL OF GLOSTER.   O madam, my old heart is cracked, it's cracked!

REGAN.   What, did my father's godson seek your life?

He whom my father named? Your Edgar?

EARL OF GLOSTER.   O lady, lady, shame would have it hid!

REGAN.   Was he not companion with the riotous knights

That tend upon my father?

EARL OF GLOSTER.   I know not, madam. 'Tis too bad, too bad!

EDMUND.   Yes, madam, he was of that consort.

REGAN.   No marvel then though he were ill affected.

'Tis they have put him on the old man's death,

To have th' expense and waste of his revenues.

全国的人都可以注意他。我的孝顺的孩子，你不学你哥哥的坏样，我一定想法子使你能够承继我的土地。

（康华尔、里根及侍从等上。）

康华尔：　您好，我的尊贵的朋友！我还不过刚到这儿，就已经听见了奇怪的消息。

里根：　要是真有那样的事，那罪人真是万死不足蔽辜了。是怎么一回事，伯爵？

葛罗斯特：　啊！夫人，我这颗老心已经碎了，已经碎了！

里根：　什么！我父亲的义子要谋害您的性命吗？就是我父亲替他取名字的，您的爱德伽吗？

葛罗斯特：　啊！夫人，夫人，发生了这种事情，真是说来叫人丢脸。

里根：　他不是常常跟我父亲身边的那些横行不法的骑士们在一起吗？

葛罗斯特：　我不知道，夫人。太可恶了！太可恶了！

爱德蒙：　是的，夫人，他正是常跟这些人在一起的。

里根：　无怪他会变得这样坏；一定是他们撺掇他谋害了老头子，好把他的财产拿出来给大家挥霍。今天傍晚的时候，我接到我

I have this present evening from my sister

Been well informed of them, and with such cautions

That if they come to sojourn at my house,

I'll not be there.

DUKE OF CORNWALL.   Nor I, assure thee, Regan.

Edmund, I hear that you have shown your father

A childlike office.

EDMUND.   Twas my duty, sir.

EARL OF GLOSTER.   He did bewray his practice, and received

This hurt you see, striving to apprehend him.

DUKE OF CORNWALL.   Is he pursued?

EARL OF GLOSTER.   Ay, my good lord.

DUKE OF CORNWALL.   If he be taken, he shall never more

Be feared of doing harm. Make your own purpose,

How in my strength you please. For you, Edmund,

Whose virtue and obedience doth this instant

So much commend itself, you shall be ours.

Natures of such deep trust we shall much need;

You we first seize on.

EDMUND.   I shall serve you, sir,

Truly, however else.

EARL OF GLOSTER.   For him I thank your Grace.

DUKE OF CORNWALL.   You know not why we came to visit you –

REGAN.   Thus out of season, threading dark-eyed night.

Occasions, noble Gloster, of some poise,

Wherein we must have use of your advice.

姐姐的一封信，她告诉我他们种种不法的情形，并且警告我要是他们想要住到我的家里来，我千万不要招待他们。

康华尔：　相信我，里根，我也绝不会去招待他们。爱德蒙，我听说你对你的父亲很尽孝道。

爱德蒙：　那是做儿子的本分，殿下。

葛罗斯特：　他揭发了他哥哥的阴谋；您看他身上的这一处伤就是因为他奋不顾身，想要捉住那畜生而受到的。

康华尔：　那凶徒逃走了，有没有人追上去？

葛罗斯特：　有的，殿下。

康华尔：　要是他给我们捉住了，我们一定不让他再为非作恶；你只要决定一个办法，在我的权力范围以内，我都可以替你办到。爱德蒙，你这一回所表现的深明大义的孝心，使我们十分赞美；像你这样不负托付的人，正是我们所需要的，我们将要大大地重用你。

爱德蒙：　殿下，我愿意为您尽忠效命。

葛罗斯特：　殿下这样看得起他，使我感激万分。

康华尔：　你还不知道我们现在所以要来看你的原因——

里根：　尊贵的葛罗斯特，我们这样在黑暗的夜色之中，一路摸索前来，实在是因为有一些相当重要的事情，必须请教请教您的高见。我们的父亲和姐姐都有信来，说他们两人之间发生了一

Our father he hath writ, so hath our sister, Of differences, which I best thought it fit

To answer from our home. The several messengers

From hence attend dispatch. Our good old friend,

Lay comforts to your bosom, and bestow

Your needful counsel to our business,

Which craves the instant use.

EARL OF GLOSTER.　I serve you, madam.

Your Graces are right welcome.

[*Exeunt.*]

些冲突；我想最好不要在我们自己的家里答复他们；两方面的
使者都在这儿等候我打发。我们的善良的老朋友，您不要气恼，
替我们赶快出个主意吧。

葛罗斯特：　　夫人但有所命，我总是愿意贡献我的一得之愚的。殿
下和夫人光临蓬荜，欢迎得很！（同下。）

ACT II   SCENE II

Before Gloster's Castle.

[*Enter Kent and Oswald the Steward, severally.*]

OSWALD.   Good dawning to thee, friend. Art of this house?

EARL OF KENT.   Ay.

OSWALD.   Where may we set our horses?

EARL OF KENT.   I' th' mire.

OSWALD.   Prithee, if thou lov'st me, tell me.

EARL OF KENT.   I love thee not.

OSWALD.   Why then, I care not for thee.

EARL OF KENT.   If I had thee in Lipsbury Pinfold, I would make thee
    care for me.

OSWALD.   Why dost thou use me thus? I know thee not.

EARL OF KENT.   Fellow, I know thee.

OSWALD.   What dost thou know me for? –

EARL OF KENT.   A knave; a rascal; an eater of broken meats; a base,
    proud, shallow, beggarly, three-suited, hundred-pound, filthy,
    worsted-stocking knave; a lily-livered, action-taking, whoreson,
    glass-gazing, super-serviceable, finical rogue; one-trunk-inheriting
    slave; one that wouldst be a bawd in way of good service, and art
    nothing but the composition of a knave, beggar, coward, pander,

第二幕　第二场

葛罗斯特城堡之前。
（肯特及奥斯华德各上。）

奥斯华德：　早安，朋友；你是这屋子里的人吗？

肯特：　喂。

奥斯华德：　什么地方可以让我们拴马？

肯特：　烂泥地里。

奥斯华德：　对不起，大家是好朋友，告诉我吧。

肯特：　谁是你的好朋友？

奥斯华德：　好，那么我也不理你。

肯特：　要是我把你一口咬住，看你理不理我。

奥斯华德：　你为什么对我这样？我又不认识你。

肯特：　家伙，我认识你。

奥斯华德：　你认识我是谁？

肯特：　一个无赖；一个恶棍；一个吃剩饭的家伙；一个下贱的、骄傲的、浅薄的、叫花子一样的、只有三身衣服、全部家私算起来不过一百镑的、卑鄙龌龊的、穿毛绒袜子的奴才；一个没有胆量的、靠着官府势力压人的奴才；一个婊子生的、顾影自怜的、奴颜婢膝的、涂脂抹粉的混账东西；全部家私都在一只箱子里的下流胚，一个天生的王八胚子；又是奴才，又是叫花

and the son and heir of a mongrel bitch; one whom I will beat into clamorous whining, if thou deny the least syllable of thy addition.

OSWALD.　Why, what a monstrous fellow art thou, thus to rail on one that's neither known of thee nor knows thee!

EARL OF KENT.　What a brazen-faced varlet art thou, to deny thou knowest me! Is it two days ago since I beat thee and tripped up thy heels before the King? Draw, you rogue! for, though it be night, yet the moon shines. I'll make a sop o' th' moonshine o' you. [*Draws his sword.*] Draw, you whoreson cullionly barber-monger! draw!

OSWALD.　Away! I have nothing to do with thee.

EARL OF KENT.　Draw, you rascal! You come with letters against the King, and take Vanity the puppet's part against the royalty of her father. Draw, you rogue, or I'll so carbonado your shanks! Draw, you rascal! Come your ways!

OSWALD.　Help, ho! murther! help!

EARL OF KENT.　Strike, you slave! Stand, rogue! Stand, you neat slave! Strike!

　　[*Beats him.*]

OSWALD.　Help, ho! murther! murther!

[*Enter Edmund, with his rapier drawn.*]

EDMUND.　How now? What's the matter?

　　[*Parts them.*]

子，又是懦夫，又是王八，又是一条杂种老母狗的儿子；要是你不承认你这些头衔，我要把你打得放声大哭。

奥斯华德：　咦，奇怪，你是个什么东西，你也不认识我，我也不认识你，怎么开口骂人？

肯特：　你还说不认识我，你这厚脸皮的奴才！两天以前，我不是把你踢倒在地上，还在王上的面前打过你吗？拔出剑来，你这混蛋；虽然是夜里，月亮照着呢；我要在月光底下把你剁得稀烂。（拔剑。）拔出剑来，你这婊子生的、臭打扮的下流东西，拔出剑来！

奥斯华德：　去！我不跟你胡闹。

肯特：　拔出剑来，你这恶棍！谁叫你做人家的傀儡，替一个女儿寄信攻击她的父王，还自鸣得意呢？拔出剑来，你这混蛋，否则我要砍下你的胫骨。拔出剑来，恶棍；来来来！

奥斯华德：　喂！救命哪！要杀人啦！救命哪！

肯特：　来，你这奴才；站住，混蛋，别跑；你这漂亮的奴才，你不会还手吗？（打奥斯华德。）

奥斯华德：　救命啊！要杀人啦！要杀人啦！

（爱德蒙拔剑上。）

爱德蒙：　怎么！什么事？（分开二人。）

EARL OF KENT.   With you, goodman boy, an you please! Come, I'll flesh ye! Come on, young master!

[*Enter Cornwall, Regan, Gloster, and Servents.*]

EARL OF GLOSTER.   Weapons? arms? What's the matter here?

DUKE OF CORNWALL.   Keep peace, upon your lives!
He dies that strikes again. What is the matter?

REGAN.   The messengers from our sister and the King.

DUKE OF CORNWALL.   What is your difference? Speak.

OSWALD.   I am scarce in breath, my lord.

EARL OF KENT.   No marvel, you have so bestirred your valour.
You cowardly rascal, nature disclaims in thee; a tailor made thee.

DUKE OF CORNWALL.   Thou art a strange fellow. A tailor make a man?

EARL OF KENT.   Ay, a tailor, sir. A stonecutter or a painter could not have made him so ill, though he had been but two hours at the trade.

DUKE OF CORNWALL.   Speak yet, how grew your quarrel?

OSWALD.   This ancient ruffian, sir, whose life I have spared at suit of his grey beard –

EARL OF KENT.   Thou whoreson zed! thou unnecessary letter! My lord, if you'll give me leave, I will tread this unbolted villain into mortar and daub the walls of a jakes with him. Spare my grey beard, you wagtail?

DUKE OF CORNWALL.   Peace, sirrah!

肯特：　好小子，你也要寻事吗？来，我们试一下吧！来，小哥儿。

（康华尔、里根、葛罗斯特及众仆上。）

葛罗斯特：　动刀动剑的，什么事呀？

康华尔：　大家不要闹；谁再动手，就叫他死。怎么一回事？

里根：　一个是我姐姐的使者，一个是国王的使者。

康华尔：　你们为什么争吵？说。

奥斯华德：　殿下，我给他缠得气都喘不过来啦。

肯特：　怪不得你，你把全身勇气都提起来了。你这怯懦的恶棍，
　　　　造化不承认他曾经造下你这个人；你是一个裁缝手里做出来的。

康华尔：　你是一个奇怪的家伙；一个裁缝会做出一个人来吗？

肯特：　嗯，一个裁缝；石匠或者油漆匠都不会把他做得这样坏，
　　　　即使他们学会这行手艺才不过两个钟头。

康华尔：　说，你们怎么会吵起来的？

奥斯华德：　这个老不讲理的家伙，殿下，倘不是我看在他的花白
　　　　胡子分上，早就要他的命了——

肯特：　你这婊子养的、不中用的废物！殿下，要是您允许我的话，
　　　　我要把这不成东西的流氓踏成一堆替人家涂刷茅厕的泥浆。看
　　　　在我的花白胡子分上？你这摇尾乞怜的狗！

康华尔：　住口！畜生，你规矩也不懂吗？

You beastly knave, know you no reverence?

EARL OF KENT.　　Yes, sir, but anger hath a privilege.

DUKE OF CORNWALL.　　Why art thou angry?

EARL OF KENT.　　That such a slave as this should wear a sword,

　　Who wears no honesty. Such smiling rogues as these,

　　Like rats, oft bite the holy cords atwain

　　Which are too intrinse t' unloose; smooth every passion

　　That in the natures of their lords rebel,

　　Bring oil to fire, snow to their colder moods;

　　Renege, affirm, and turn their halcyon beaks

　　With every gale and vary of their masters,

　　Knowing naught like dogs but following.

　　A plague upon your epileptic visage!

　　Smile you my speeches, as I were a fool?

　　Goose, an I had you upon Sarum Plain,

　　I'ld drive ye cackling home to Camelot.

DUKE OF CORNWALL.　　What, art thou mad, old fellow?

EARL OF GLOSTER.　　How fell you out? Say that.

EARL OF KENT.　　No contraries hold more antipathy

　　Than I and such a knave.

DUKE OF CORNWALL.　　Why dost thou call him knave? What is his fault?

EARL OF KENT.　　His countenance likes me not.

DUKE OF CORNWALL.　　No more perchance does mine, or his, or hers.

EARL OF KENT.　　Sir, 'tis my occupation to be plain.

肯特：　是，殿下；可是我实在气愤不过，也就顾不得了。

康华尔：　你为什么气愤？

肯特：　我气愤的是像这样一个奸诈的奴才，居然也让他佩起剑来。都是这种笑脸的小人，像老鼠一样咬破了神圣的伦常纲纪；他们的主上起了一个恶念，他们便竭力逢迎，不是火上浇油，就是雪上添霜；他们最擅长的是随风转舵，他们的主人说一声是，他们也跟着说是，说一声不，他们也跟着说不，就像狗一样什么都不知道，只知道跟着主人跑。恶疮烂掉了你的抽搐的面孔！你笑我所说的话，你以为我是个傻瓜吗？呆鹅，要是我在旷野里碰见了你，看我不把你打得嘎嘎乱叫，一路赶回你的老家去！

康华尔：　什么！你疯了吗，老头儿？

葛罗斯特：　说，你们究竟是怎么吵起来的？

肯特：　我跟这混蛋是势不两立的。

康华尔：　你为什么叫他混蛋？他做错了什么事？

肯特：　我不喜欢他的面孔。

康华尔：　也许你也不喜欢我的面孔、他的面孔，还有她的面孔。

肯特：　殿下，我是说惯老实话的；我曾经见过一些面孔，比现在

I have seen better faces in my time

Than stands on any shoulder that I see

Before me at this instant.

DUKE OF CORNWALL.   This is some fellow

Who, having been praised for bluntness, doth affect

A saucy roughness, and constrains the garb

Quite from his nature. He cannot flatter, he!

An honest mind and plain – he must speak truth!

An they will take it, so; if not, he's plain.

These kind of knaves I know which in this plainness

Harbour more craft and more corrupter ends

Than twenty silly-ducking observant

That stretch their duties nicely.

EARL OF KENT.   Sir, in good faith, in sincere verity,

Under th' allowance of your great aspect,

Whose influence, like the wreath of radiant fire

On flickering Phoebus' front –

DUKE OF CORNWALL.   What mean'st by this?

EARL OF KENT.   To go out of my dialect, which you discommend so

much. I know, sir, I am no flatterer. He that beguiled you in a plain

accent was a plain knave, which, for my part, I will not be, though I

should win your displeasure to entreat me to't.

DUKE OF CORNWALL.   What was th' offence you gave him?

OSWALD.   I never gave him any.

It pleased the King his master very late

To strike at me, upon his misconstruction;

站在我面前的这些面孔好得多啦。

康华尔：　这个人正是那种因为有人称赞了他的言辞率直，就此装
出一副粗鲁的、目中无人的样子，一味矫揉造作，仿佛他生来
就是这样一个家伙。他不会谄媚，他有一颗正直坦白的心，他
必须说老实话；要是人家愿意接受他的意见，很好；不然的话，
他是个老实人。我知道这种家伙，他们用坦白的外表，包藏着
极大的奸谋祸心，比二十个胁肩谄笑、小心翼翼的愚蠢的谄媚
者更要不怀好意。

肯特：　殿下，您的伟大的明鉴，就像福玻斯神光煜煜的额上的烨
耀的火轮，请您照临我的善意的忠诚，恳切的虔心——

康华尔：　这是什么意思？

肯特：　因为您不喜欢我的话，所以我改变了一个样子。我知道我
不是一个谄媚之徒；我也不愿做一个故意用率直的言语诱惑人
家听信的奸诈小人；即使您请求我做这样的人，我也不怕得罪
您，绝不从命。

康华尔：　（向奥斯华德）你在什么地方冒犯了他？

奥斯华德：　我从来没有冒犯过他。最近王上因为对我有了点误会，
把我殴打；他便助主为虐，闪在我的背后把我踢倒地上，侮辱
谩骂，无所不至，装出一副非常勇敢的神气；他的王上看见他

When he, conjunct, and flattering his displeasure,

Tripped me behind; being down, insulted, railed

And put upon him such a deal of man

That worthied him, got praises of the King

For him attempting who was self-subdued;

And, in the fleshment of this dread exploit,

Drew on me here again.

EARL OF KENT.　None of these rogues and cowards

But Ajax is their fool.

DUKE OF CORNWALL.　Fetch forth the stocks!

You stubborn ancient knave, you reverent braggart,

We'll teach you –

EARL OF KENT.　Sir, I am too old to learn.

Call not your stocks for me. I serve the King;

On whose employment I was sent to you.

You shall do small respect, show too bold malice

Against the grace and person of my master,

Stocking his messenger.

DUKE OF CORNWALL.　Fetch forth the stocks! As I have life and honour,

There shall he sit till noon.

REGAN.　Till noon? Till night, my lord, and all night too!

EARL OF KENT.　Why, madam, if I were your father's dog,

You should not use me so.

REGAN.　Sir, being his knave, I will.

DUKE OF CORNWALL.　This is a fellow of the selfsame colour

这样，把他称赞了两句，我又极力克制自己，他便得意忘形，以为我不是他的对手，所以一看见我，又拔剑跟我闹起来了。

肯特：　和这些流氓和懦夫相比，埃阿斯只能当他们的傻子。

康华尔：　拿足柳来！你这口出狂言的倔强的老贼，我们要教训你一下。

肯特：　殿下，我已经太老，不能受您的教训了；您不能用足柳柳我。我是王上的人，奉他的命令前来；您要是把他的使者柳起来，那未免对我的主上太失敬、太放肆无礼了。

康华尔：　拿足柳来！凭着我的生命和荣誉起誓，他必须锁在足柳里直到中午为止。

里根：　到中午为止！到晚上，殿下；把他整整柳上一夜再说。

肯特：　啊，夫人，假如我是您父亲的狗，您也不该这样对待我。

里根：　因为你是他的奴才，所以我要这样对待你。

康华尔：　这正是我们的姐姐说起的那个家伙。来，拿足柳来。（从

Our sister speaks of. Come, bring away the stocks!

[*Stocks brought out.*]

EARL OF GLOSTER.   Let me beseech your Grace not to do so.

His fault is much, and the good King his master

Will check him for't. Your purposed low correction

Is such as basest and contemnedest wretches

For pilf'rings and most common trespasses

Are punished with. The King must take it ill

That he, so slightly valued in his messenger,

Should have him thus restrained.

DUKE OF CORNWALL.   I'll answer that.

REGAN.   My sister may receive it much more worse,

To have her gentleman abused, assaulted,

For following her affairs. Put in his legs. –

[*Kent is put in the stocks.*]

Come, my good lord, away.

[*Exeunt all but Gloster and Kent.*]

EARL OF GLOSTER.   I am sorry for thee, friend. 'Tis the Duke's pleasure,

Whose disposition, all the world well knows,

Will not berubbed nor stopped. I'll entreat for thee.

EARL OF KENT.   Pray do not, sir. I have watched and travelled hard.

Some time I shall sleep out, the rest I'll whistle.

A good man's fortune may grow out at heels.

Give you good morrow!

仆取出足枷。）

葛罗斯特：　殿下，请您不要这样。他的过失诚然很大，王上知道了一定会责罚他的；您所决定的这一种羞辱的刑罚，只能惩戒那些犯偷窃之类普通小罪的下贱的囚徒；他是王上差来的人，要是您给他这样的处分，王上一定要认为您轻蔑了他的来使而心中不快。

康华尔：　那我可以负责。

里根：　我的姐姐要是知道她的使者因为奉行她的命令而被人这样侮辱殴打，她的心里还要不高兴哩。把他的腿放进去。（从仆将肯特套入足枷。）来，殿下，我们走吧。（除葛罗斯特、肯特外均下。）

葛罗斯特：　朋友，我很为你抱憾；这是公爵的意思，全世界都知道他的脾气非常固执，不肯接受人家的劝阻。我还要替你向他求情。

肯特：　请您不必多此一举，大人。我走了许多路，还没有睡过觉；一部分的时间将在瞌睡中过去，醒着的时候我可以吹吹口哨。好人上足枷，因此就走好运也说不定呢。再会！

EARL OF GLOSTER.   The Duke 's to blame in this; 'twill be ill taken.

[*Exit.*]

EARL OF KENT.   Good King, that must approve the common saw,

Thou out of heaven's benediction com'st

To the warm sun!

Approach, thou beacon to this under globe,

That by thy comfortable beams I may

Peruse this letter. Nothing almost sees miracles

But misery. I know 'tis from Cordelia,

Who hath most fortunately been informed

Of my obscured course – and shall find time

From this enormous state, seeking to give

Losses their remedies – All weary and o'erwatched,

Take vantage, heavy eyes, not to behold

This shameful lodging.

Fortune, good night; smile once more, turn thy wheel.

[*Sleeps.*]

葛罗斯特：　这是公爵的不是；王上一定会见怪的。（下。）

肯特：　好王上，你正像俗语说的，抛下天堂的幸福，来受赤日的煎熬了。来吧，你这照耀下土的炬火，让我借着你的温柔的光辉，可以读一读这封信。只有倒霉的人才会遇见奇迹；我知道这是考狄利娅寄来的，我的改头换面的行踪，已经侥幸给她知道了；她一定会找到一个机会，纠正这种反常的情形。疲倦得很；闭上了吧，沉重的眼睛，免得看见你自己的耻辱。晚安，命运，求你转过你的轮子来，再向我们微笑吧。（睡。）

ACT II   SCENE III

The open country.
[Enter Edgar.]

EDGAR.   I heard myself proclaimed,
　　　And by the happy hollow of a tree
　　　Escaped the hunt. No port is free, no place
　　　That guard and most unusual vigilance
　　　Does not attend my taking. Whiles I may scape,
　　　I will preserve myself; and am bethought
　　　To take the basest and most poorest shape
　　　That ever penury, in contempt of man,
　　　Brought near to beast. My face I'll grime with filth,
　　　Blanket my loins, elf all my hair in knots,
　　　And with presented nakedness outface
　　　The winds and persecutions of the sky.
　　　The country gives me proof and precedent
　　　Of Bedlam beggars, who, with roaring voices,
　　　Strike in their numbed and mortified bare arms
　　　Pins, wooden pricks, nails, sprigs of rosemary;
　　　And with this horrible object, from low farms,
　　　Poor pelting villages, sheep-cotes, and mills,

第二幕　第三场

荒野的一部。

（爱德伽上。）

爱德伽：　　听说他们已经发出告示捉我；幸亏我躲在一株空心的树
干里，没有给他们找到。没有一处城门可以出入无阻；没有一
个地方不是警卫森严，准备把我捉住！我总得设法逃过人家的
耳目，保全自己的生命；我想还不如改扮做一个最卑贱穷苦、
最为世人所轻视、和禽兽相去无几的家伙；我要用污泥涂在脸
上，一块毡布裹住我的腰，把满头的头发打了许多乱结，赤身
裸体，抵抗着风雨的侵凌。这地方本来有许多疯丐，他们高声
叫喊，用针哪、木锥哪、钉子哪、迷迭香的树枝哪，刺在他们
麻木而僵硬的手臂上；用这种可怕的形状，到那些穷苦的农场、
乡村、羊棚和磨坊里去，有时候发出一些疯狂的诅咒，有时候
向人哀求祈祷，乞讨一些布施。我现在学着他们的样子，一定
不会引起人家的疑心。可怜的疯叫花！可怜的汤姆！倒有几分
像；我现在不再是爱德伽了。（下。）

Sometime with lunatic bans, sometime with prayers,

Enforce their charity. Poor Turlygod! poor Tom!

That's something yet! Edgar I nothing am.

[*Exit.*]

ACT II   SCENE IV

Before Gloster's Castle; Kent in the stocks.
[Enter Lear, Fool, and Gentleman.]

KING LEAR.   Tis strange that they should so depart from home,

And not send back my messenger.

GENTLEMAN.   As I learned,

The night before there was no purpose in them

Of this remove.

EARL OF KENT.   Hail to thee, noble master!

KING LEAR.   Ha!

Mak'st thou this shame thy pastime?

EARL OF KENT.   No, my lord.

FOOL.   Ha, ha! look! he wears cruel garters. Horses are tied by the head, dogs and bears by th' neck, monkeys by th' loins, and men by th' legs. When a man's over-lusty at legs, then he wears wooden nether-stocks.

KING LEAR.   What's he that hath so much thy place mistook

To set thee here?

EARL OF KENT.   It is both he and she – Your son and daughter.

KING LEAR.   No.

EARL OF KENT.   Yes.

第二幕　第四场

葛罗斯特城堡前。肯特系足枷中。

（李尔、弄人及侍臣上。）

李尔：　　真奇怪，他们不在家里，又不打发我的使者回去。

侍臣：　　我听说他们在前一个晚上还不曾有走动的意思。

肯特：　　祝福您，尊贵的主人！

李尔：　　嘿！你把这样的羞辱作为消遣吗？

肯特：　　不，陛下。

弄人：　　哈哈！他吊着一副多么难受的袜带！缚马缚在头上，缚狗
　　　　　缚熊缚在脖子上，缚猴子缚在腰上，缚人缚在腿上；一个人的
　　　　　腿儿太会活动了，就要叫他穿木袜子。

李尔：　　谁认错了人，把你锁在这儿？

肯特：　　是那一对男女——您的女婿和女儿。

李尔：　　不。

肯特：　　是的。

KING LEAR.　　No, I say.

EARL OF KENT.　　I say yea.

KING LEAR.　　No, no, they would not!

EARL OF KENT.　　Yes, they have.

KING LEAR.　　By Jupiter, I swear no!

EARL OF KENT.　　By Juno, I swear ay!

KING LEAR.　　They durst not do't;

　　　　They would not, could not do't. 'Tis worse than murther

　　　　To do upon respect such violent outrage.

　　　　Resolve me with all modest haste which way

　　　　Thou mightst deserve or they impose this usage,

　　　　Coming from us.

EARL OF KENT.　　My lord, when at their home

　　　　I did commend your Highness' letters to them,

　　　　Ere I was risen from the place that showed

　　　　My duty kneeling, came there a reeking post,

　　　　Stewed in his haste, half breathless, panting forth

　　　　From Goneril his mistress salutations;

　　　　Delivered letters, spite of intermission,

　　　　Which presently they read; on whose contents,

　　　　They summoned up their meiny, straight took horse,

　　　　Commanded me to follow and attend

　　　　The leisure of their answer, gave me cold looks,

　　　　And meeting here the other messenger,

　　　　Whose welcome I perceived had poisoned mine –

　　　　Being the very fellow which of late

李尔：　我说不。

肯特：　我说是的。

李尔：　不，不，他们不会干这样的事。

肯特：　他们干也干了。

李尔：　凭着朱庇特起誓，没有这样的事。

肯特：　凭着朱诺起誓，有这样的事。

李尔：　他们不敢做这样的事；他们不能，也不会做这样的事；要是他们有意作出这种重大的暴行来，那简直比杀人更不可恕了。赶快告诉我，你究竟犯了什么罪，他们才会用这种刑罚来对待一个国王的使者。

肯特：　陛下，我带了您的信到了他们家里，当我跪在地上把信交上去，还没有立起身来的时候，又有一个使者汗流满面，气喘吁吁，急急忙忙地奔了进来，代他的女主人高纳里尔向他们请安，随后把一封书信递上去，打断了我的公事；他们看见她也有信来，就来不及理睬我，先读她的信；读罢了信，他们立刻召集仆从，上马出发，叫我跟到这儿来，等候他们的答复；对待我十分冷淡。一到这儿，我又碰见了那个使者，他也就是最近对您非常无礼的那个家伙，我知道他们对我这样冷淡，都是因为他来了的缘故，一时激于气愤，不加考虑地向他动起武来；他看见我这样，就高声发出怯懦的叫喊，惊动了全宅子的人。您的女婿女儿认为我犯了这样的罪，应该把我羞辱一下，所以就把我枷起来了。

Displayed so saucily against your Highness –

Having more man than wit about me, drew.

He raised the house with loud and coward cries.

Your son and daughter found this trespass worth

The shame which here it suffers.

FOOL.   Winter's not gone yet, if the wild geese fly that way.

Fathers that wear rags

Do make their children blind;

But fathers that bear bags

Shall see their children kind.

Fortune, that arrant whore,

Ne'er turns the key to th' poor.

But for all this, thou shalt have as many dolours for thy daughters

as thou canst tell in a year.

KING LEAR.   O, how this mother swells up toward my heart!

Hysterica passio! Down, thou climbing sorrow!

Thy element's below! Where is this daughter?

EARL OF KENT.   With the Earl, sir, here within.

KING LEAR.   Follow me not; Stay here.

    [*Exit.*]

GENTLEMAN.   Made you no more offence but what you speak of?

EARL OF KENT.   None.

How chance the King comes with so small a number?

FOOL.   An thou hadst been set i' th' stocks for that question, thou

hadst well deserved it.

弄人：　冬天还没有过去，要是野雁尽往那个方向飞。

　　　　老父衣百结，

　　　　儿女不相识；

　　　　老父满囊金，

　　　　儿女尽孝心。

　　　　命运如娼妓，

　　　　贫贱遭遗弃。

　　　　虽然这样说，你的女儿们还要孝敬你数不清的烦恼哩。

李尔：　啊！我这一肚子的气都涌上我的心头来了！你这一股无名
　　　　的气恼，快给我平下去吧！我这女儿呢？

肯特：　在里边，陛下；跟伯爵在一起。

李尔：　不要跟我；在这儿等着。（下。）

侍臣：　除了你刚才所说的以外，你没有犯其他的过失吗？

肯特：　没有。王上怎么不多带几个人来？

弄人：　你会发出这么一个问题，活该给人用足枷枷起来。

EARL OF KENT.   Why, fool?

FOOL.   We'll set thee to school to an ant, to teach thee there's no
labouring i' th' winter. All that follow their noses are led by their
eyes but blind men, and there's not a nose among twenty but can
smell him that's stinking. Let go thy hold when a great wheel runs
down a hill, lest it break thy neck with following it; but the great
one that goes upward, let him draw thee after. When a wise man
gives thee better counsel, give me mine again. I would have none
but knaves follow it, since a fool gives it.

That sir which serves and seeks for gain,

And follows but for form,

Will pack when it begins to rain

And leave thee in the storm.

But I will tarry; the fool will stay,

And let the wise man fly.

The knave turns fool that runs away;

The fool no knave, perdy.

EARL OF KENT.   Where learned you this, fool?

FOOL.   Not i' th' stocks, fool.

[*Enter Lear and Gloster.*]

KING LEAR.   Deny to speak with me?

They are sick? they are weary? They have travelled all the night?
Mere fetches –

The images of revolt and flying off!

肯特：　　为什么，傻瓜？

弄人：　　你应该拜蚂蚁做老师，让它教训你冬天是不能工作的。谁
　　　　　都长着眼睛，除非瞎子，每个人都看得清自己该朝哪一边走；
　　　　　就算眼睛瞎了，二十个鼻子里也没有一个鼻子嗅不出来他身上
　　　　　发霉的味道。一个大车轮滚下山坡的时候，你千万不要抓住它，
　　　　　免得跟它一起滚下去，跌断了你的头颈；可是你要是看见它上
　　　　　山去，那么让它拖着你一起上去吧。倘然有什么聪明人给你更
　　　　　好的教训，请你把这番话还我；一个傻瓜的教训，只配让一个
　　　　　混蛋去遵从。

　　　　　他为了自己的利益，

　　　　　向你屈节卑躬，

　　　　　天色一变就要告别，

　　　　　留下你在雨中。

　　　　　聪明的人全都飞散，

　　　　　只剩傻瓜一个；

　　　　　傻瓜逃走变成混蛋，

　　　　　那混蛋不是我。

肯特：　　傻瓜，你从什么地方学会这支歌儿？

弄人：　　不是在足枷里，傻瓜。

（李尔偕葛罗斯特重上。）

李尔：　　拒绝跟我说话！他们有病！他们疲倦了，他们昨天晚上走
　　　　　路辛苦！都是些鬼话，明明是要背叛我的意思。给我再去向他
　　　　　们要一个好一点的答复来。

Fetch me a better answer.

EARL OF GLOSTER.　My dear lord,

　　You know the fiery quality of the Duke,

　　How unremovable and fixed he is

　　In his own course.

KING LEAR.　Vengeance! plague! death! confusion!

　　Fiery? What quality? Why, Gloster, Gloster,

　　I'ld speak with the Duke of Cornwall and his wife.

EARL OF GLOSTER.　Well, my good lord, I have informed them so.

KING LEAR.　Informed them? Dost thou understand me, man?

EARL OF GLOSTER.　Ay, my good lord.

KING LEAR.　The King would speak with Cornwall; the dear father

　　Would with his daughter speak, commands her service.

　　Are they informed of this? My breath and blood!

　　Fiery? the fiery Duke? Tell the hot Duke that –

　　No, but not yet! May be he is not well.

　　Infirmity doth still neglect all office

　　Whereto our health is bound. We are not ourselves

　　When nature, being oppressed, commands the mind

　　To suffer with the body. I'll forbear;

　　And am fallen out with my more headier will,

　　To take the indisposed and sickly fit

　　For the sound man. –Death on my state! Wherefore

　　Should be sit here? This act persuades me

　　That this remotion of the Duke and her

　　Is practice only. Give me my servant forth.

葛罗斯特：　　陛下，您知道公爵的火性，他决定了怎样就是怎样，再也没有更改的。

李尔：　　报应哪！疫疠！死亡！祸乱！火性！什么火性？嘿，葛罗斯特，葛罗斯特，我要跟康华尔公爵和他的妻子说话。

葛罗斯特：　　呃，陛下，我已经对他们说过了。

李尔：　　对他们说过了！你懂得我的意思吗？

葛罗斯特：　　是，陛下。

李尔：　　国王要跟康华尔说话；亲爱的父亲要跟他的女儿说话，叫她出来见我：你有没有这样告诉他们？我这口气，我这一腔血！哼，火性！火性子的公爵！对那性如烈火的公爵说——不，且慢，也许他真的不大舒服；一个人为了疾病往往疏忽了他原来健康时的责任，是应当加以原谅的；我们身体上有了病痛，精神上总是连带觉得烦躁郁闷，那时候就不由我们自己做主了。我且忍耐一下，不要太鲁莽了，对一个有病的人作过分求全的责备。该死！（视肯特。）为什么把他枷在这儿？这一种举动使我相信公爵和她对我回避，完全是一种预定的计谋。把我的仆人放出来还我。去，对公爵和他的妻子说，我现在立刻就要跟他们说话；叫他们赶快出来见我，否则我要在他们的寝室门前擂起鼓来，搅得他们不能安睡。

Go tell the Duke and 's wife I'd speak with them –
Now, presently. Bid them come forth and hear me,
Or at their chamber door I'll beat the drum
Till it cry sleep to death.

EARL OF GLOSTER.   I would have all well betwixt you.
  [*Exit.*]

KING LEAR.   O me, my heart, my rising heart! But down!

FOOL.   Cry to it, nuncle, as the cockney did to the eels when she
  put 'em i' th' paste alive. She knapped 'em o' th' coxcombs with a
  stick and cried, Down, wantons, down! 'Twas her brother that, in
  pure kindness to his horse, buttered his hay.

[*Enter Cornwall, Regan, Gloster, Servants.*]

KING LEAR.   Good morrow to you both.

DUKE OF CORNWALL.   Hail to your Grace!
  [*Kent here set at liberty.*]

REGAN.   I am glad to see your Highness.

KING LEAR.   Regan, I think you are; I know what reason
  I have to think so. If thou shouldst not be glad,
  I would divorce me from thy mother's tomb,
  Sepulchring an adultress.
  [*To Kent.*] O, are you free?
  Some other time for that. – Beloved Regan,
  Thy sister's naught. O Regan, she hath tied

葛罗斯特：　我但愿你们大家和和好好的。（下。）

李尔：　啊！我的心！我的怒气直冲的心！把怒气退下去吧！

弄人：　你向它吆喝吧，老伯伯，就像厨娘把活鳗鱼放进面糊里的时候那样；她拿起手里的棍子，在它们的头上敲了几下，喊道："下去，坏东西，下去！"也就像她的兄弟，为了爱他的马儿，替它在草料上涂了牛油。

（康华尔、里根、葛罗斯特及众仆上。）

李尔：　你们两位早安！

康华尔：　祝福陛下！

　　　（众人释肯特。）

里根：　我很高兴看见陛下。

李尔：　里根，我想你一定高兴看见我的；我知道我为什么要这样想；要是你不高兴看见我，我就要跟你已故的母亲离婚，把她的坟墓当做一座淫妇的丘陇。（向肯特）啊！你放出来了吗？等会儿再谈吧。亲爱的里根，你的姐姐太不孝啦。啊，里根！她的无情的凶恶像饿鹰的利喙一样猛啄我的心。（以手按于心口。）我简直不能告诉你；你不会相信她忍心害理到什么地步——啊，里根！

Sharp-toothed unkindness, like a vulture, here!

[*Lays his hand on his heart.*]

I can scarce speak to thee. Thou'lt not believe

Of how depraved a quality – O Regan!

REGAN.   I pray you, sir, take patience. I have hope

You less know how to value her desert

Than she to scant her duty.

KING LEAR.   Say, how is that?

REGAN.   I cannot think my sister in the least

Would fail her obligation. If, sir, perchance

She have restrained the riots of your followers,

'Tis on such ground, and to such wholesome end,

As clears her from all blame.

KING LEAR.   My curses on her!

REGAN.   O, sir, you are old!

Nature in you stands on the very verge

Of her confine. You should be ruled, and led

By some discretion that discerns your state

Better than you yourself. Therefore I pray you

That to our sister you do make return;

Say you have wronged her, sir.

KING LEAR.   Ask her forgiveness?

Do you but mark how this becomes the house:

Dear daughter, I confess that I am old.

[*Kneels.*]

Age is unnecessary. On my knees I beg

里根：　　父亲，请您不要恼怒。我想她不会对您有失敬礼，恐怕还是您不能谅解她的苦心哩。

李尔：　　啊，这是什么意思？

里根：　　我想我的姐姐绝不会有什么地方不尽孝道；要是，父亲，她约束了您那班随从的放荡的行为，那当然有充分的理由和正大的目的，绝对不能怪她的。

李尔：　　我的诅咒降在她的头上！

里根：　　啊，父亲！您年纪老了，已经快到了生命的尽头；应该让一个比您自己更明白您的地位的人管教管教您；所以我劝您还是回到姐姐的地方去，对她赔一个不是。

李尔：　　请求她的饶恕吗？你看这样像不像个样子：“好女儿，我承认我年纪老，不中用啦，让我跪在地上，（跪下。）请求您赏给我几件衣服穿，赏给我一张床睡，赏给我一些东西吃吧。”

That you'll vouchsafe me raiment, bed, and food.'

REGAN.　Good sir, no more! These are unsightly tricks.

Return you to my sister.

KING LEAR.　[*Rises.*] Never, Regan!

She hath abated me of half my train;

Looked black upon me; struck me with her tongue,

Most serpent-like, upon the very heart.

All the stored vengeances of heaven fall

On her ingrateful top! Strike her young bones,

You taking airs, with lameness!

DUKE OF CORNWALL.　Fie, sir, fie!

KING LEAR.　You nimble lightnings, dart your blinding flames

Into her scornful eyes! Infect her beauty,

You fen-sucked fogs, drawn by the powerful sun,

To fall and blast her pride!

REGAN.　O the blest gods!So will you wish on me.

When the rash mood is on.

KING LEAR.　No, Regan, thou shalt never have my curse.

Thy tender-hefted nature shall not give

Thee o'er to harshness. Her eyes are fierce; but thine

Do comfort, and not burn. 'Tis not in thee

To grudge my pleasures, to cut off my train,

To bandy hasty words, to scant my sizes,

And, in conclusion, to oppose the bolt

Against my coming in. Thou better know'st

The offices of nature, bond of childhood,

里根：　父亲，别这样子；这算个什么，简直是胡闹！回到我姐姐
　　　那儿去吧。

李尔：　（起立。）再也不回去了，里根。她裁撤了我一半的侍从；
　　　不给我好脸看；用她的毒蛇一样的舌头打击我的心。但愿上天
　　　蓄积的愤怒一起降在她的无情无义的头上！但愿恶风吹打她的
　　　腹中的胎儿，让它生下地来就是个瘸子！

康华尔：　嘿！这是什么话！

李尔：　迅疾的闪电啊，把你的炫目的火焰，射进她的傲慢的眼睛
　　　里去吧！在烈日的熏灼下蒸发起来的沼地的瘴气啊，损坏她的
　　　美貌，毁灭她的骄傲吧！

里根：　天上的神明啊！您要是对我发起怒来，也会这样咒我的。

李尔：　不，里根，你永远不会受我的诅咒；你的温柔的天性绝不
　　　会使你干出冷酷残忍的行为来。她的眼睛里有一股凶光，可是
　　　你的眼睛却是温存而和蔼的。你绝不会吝惜我的享受，裁撤我
　　　的侍从，用不逊之言向我顶嘴，削减我的费用，甚至于把我关
　　　在门外不让我进来；你是懂得天伦的义务、儿女的责任、孝敬
　　　的礼貌和受恩的感激的；你总还没有忘记我曾经赐给你一半的
　　　国土。

Effects of courtesy, dues of gratitude.

Thy half o' th' kingdom hast thou not forgot,

Wherein I thee endowed.

REGAN.　　Good Sir,to the purpose.

KING LEAR.　　Who put my man i' th' stocks?

　　[*Tucket within.*]

DUKE OF CORNWALL.　　What trumpet's that?

REGAN.　　I know't – my sister's. This approves her letter,

　　That she would soon be here.

[*Enter Oswald the Steward.*]

REGAN.　　Is your lady come?

KING LEAR.　　This is a slave, whose easy-borrowed pride

　　Dwells in the fickle grace of her he follows.

　　Out, varlet, from my sight!

DUKE OF CORNWALL.　　What means your Grace?

KING LEAR.　　Who stocked my servant? Regan, I have good hope

　　Thou didst not know on't. –Who comes here? O heavens!

　　[*Enter Goneril.*]

　　If you do love old men, if your sweet sway

　　Allow obedience – if yourselves are old,

　　Make it your cause! Send down, and take my part!

　　[*To Goneril.*] Art not ashamed to look upon this beard? –

　　O Regan, wilt thou take her by the hand?

里根：　　父亲，不要把话说远了。

李尔：　　谁把我的人枷起来？

　　　　（内喇叭奏花腔。）

康华尔：　那是什么喇叭声音？

里根：　　我知道，是我的姐姐来了；她信上说就要到这儿来的。

（奥斯华德上。）

里根：　　夫人来了吗？

李尔：　　这是一个靠着主妇暂时的恩宠、狐假虎威、倚势凌人的奴才。滚开，贱奴，不要让我看见你！

康华尔：　陛下，这是什么意思？

李尔：　　谁把我的仆人枷起来？里根，我希望你并不知道这件事。谁来啦？（高纳里尔上。）天啊，要是你爱老人，要是凭着你统治人间的仁爱，你认为子女应该孝顺他们的父母，要是你自己也是老人，那么不要漠然无动于衷，降下你的愤怒来，帮我伸雪我的怨恨吧！（向高纳里尔）你看见我这一把胡须，不觉得惭愧吗？啊里根，你愿意跟她握手吗？

GONERIL.　Why not by th' hand, sir? How have I offended?

All's not offence that indiscretion finds

And dotage terms so.

KING LEAR.　O sides, you are too tough! Will you yet hold? How

came my man i' th' stocks?

DUKE OF CORNWALL.　I set him there, sir; but his own disorders

Deserved much less advancement.

KING LEAR.　You? Did you?

REGAN.　I pray you, father, being weak, seem so.

If, till the expiration of your month,

You will return and sojourn with my sister,

Dismissing half your train, come then to me.

I am now from home, and out of that provision

Which shall be needful for your entertainment.

KING LEAR.　Return to her, and fifty men dismissed?

No, rather I abjure all roofs, and choose

To wage against the enmity o' th' air,

To be a comrade with the wolf and owl –

Necessity's sharp pinch! Return with her?

Why, the hot-blooded France, that dowerless took

Our youngest born, I could as well be brought

To knee his throne, and, squire – like, pension beg

To keep base life afoot. Return with her?

Persuade me rather to be slave and sumpter

To this detested groom.

[*Points at Oswald.*]

高纳里尔：　为什么她不能跟我握手呢！我干了什么错事？难道凭着一张糊涂昏悖的嘴里的胡言乱语，就可以成立我的罪案吗？

李尔：　啊，我的胸膛！你还没有胀破吗？我的人怎么给你们枷了起来？

康华尔：　陛下，是我把他枷在那儿的；照他狂妄的行为，这样的惩戒还太轻呢。

李尔：　你！是你干的事吗？

里根：　父亲，您该明白您是一个衰弱的老人，一切只好将就点儿。要是您现在仍旧回去跟姐姐住在一起，裁撤了您的一半的侍从，那么等住满了一个月，再到我这儿来吧。我现在不在自己家里，要供养您也有许多不便。

李尔：　回到她那儿去？裁撤五十名侍从！不，我宁愿什么屋子也不要住，过着风餐露宿的生活，和无情的大自然抗争，和豺狼鸱鸮做伴侣，忍受一切饥寒的痛苦！回去跟她住在一起？嘿，我宁愿到那娶了我的没有嫁妆的小女儿去的热情的法兰西国王的座前匍匐膝行，像一个臣仆一样向他讨一份微薄的恩俸，苟延残喘下去。回去跟她住在一起！你还是劝我在这可恶的仆人手下当奴才、当牛马吧。（指奥斯华德。）

GONERIL.　At your choice, sir.

KING LEAR.　I prithee, daughter, do not make me mad.

　　I will not trouble thee, my child; farewell.

　　We'll no more meet, no more see one another.

　　But yet thou art my flesh, my blood, my daughter;

　　Or rather a disease that's in my flesh,

　　Which I must needs call mine. Thou art a boil,

　　A plague sore, an embossed carbuncle

　　In my corrupted blood. But I'll not chide thee.

　　Let shame come when it will,

　　I do not call it.I do not bid the Thunder-bearer shoot

　　Nor tell tales of thee to high-judging Jove.

　　Mend when thou canst; be better at thy leisure;

　　I can be patient, I can stay with Regan,

　　I and my hundred knights.

REGAN.　Not altogether so.

　　I looked not for you yet, nor am provided

　　For your fit welcome. Give ear, sir, to my sister;

　　For those that mingle reason with your passion

　　Must be content to think you old, and so –

　　But she knows what she does.

KING LEAR.　Is this well spoken?

REGAN.　I dare avouch it, sir. What, fifty followers?

　　Is it not well? What should you need of more?

　　Yea, or so many, sith that both charge and danger

　　Speak 'gainst so great a number? How in one house

高纳里尔：　随你的便。

李尔：　女儿，请你不要使我发疯；我也不愿再来打扰你了，我的
孩子。再会吧；我们从此不再相见。可是你是我的肉、我的血、
我的女儿；或者还不如说是我身体上的一个恶瘤，我不能不承
认你是我的；你是我的腐败的血液里的一个疖子、一个淤块、
一个肿毒的疔疮。可是我不愿责骂你；让羞辱自己降临你的身
上吧，我没有呼召它；我不要求天雷把你殛死，我也不把你的
忤逆向垂察善恶的天神控诉，你回去仔细想一想，趁早痛改前
非，还来得及。我可以忍耐；我可以带着我的一百个骑士，跟
里根住在一起。

里根：　那绝对不行；现在还轮不到我，我也没有预备好招待您的
礼数。父亲，听我姐姐的话吧；人家冷眼看着您这种愤怒的神
气，他们心里都要说您因为老了，所以——可是姐姐是知道她
自己该怎样做的。

李尔：　这是你的好意的劝告吗？

里根：　是的，父亲，这是我的真诚的意见。什么！五十个卫士？
这不是很好吗？再多一些有什么用处？就是这么许多人，数目
也不少了，别说供养他们不起，而且让他们成群结党，也是一
件危险的事。一间屋子里养了这许多人，受着两个主人支配，

Should many people, under two commands,

Hold amity? 'Tis hard; almost impossible.

GONERIL.   Why might not you, my lord, receive attendance

From those that she calls servants, or from mine?

REGAN.   Why not, my lord? If then they chanced to slack you,

We could control them. If you will come to me

For now I spy a danger, I entreat you

To bring but five-and-twenty. To no more

Will I give place or notice.

KING LEAR.   I gave you all –

REGAN.   And in good time you gave it!

KING LEAR.   Made you my guardians, my depositaries;

But kept a reservation to be followed

With such a number. What, must I come to you

With five-and-twenty, Regan? Said you so?

REGAN.   And speak't again my lord. No more with me.

KING LEAR.   Those wicked creatures yet do look well-favoured

When others are more wicked; not being the worst

Stands in some rank of praise. [*To Goneril.*] I'll go with thee.

Thy fifty yet doth double five-and-twenty,

And thou art twice her love.

GONERIL.   Hear, me, my lord.

What need you five-and-twenty, ten, or five,

To follow in a house where twice so many

Have a command to tend you?

REGAN.   What need one?

怎么不会发生争闹？简直不成话。

高纳里尔：　父亲，您为什么不让我们的仆人侍候您呢？

里根：　对了，父亲，那不是很好吗？要是他们怠慢了您，我们也可以训斥他们。您下回到我这儿来的时候，请您只带二十五个人来，因为现在我已经看到了一个危险；超过这个数目，我是恕不招待的。

李尔：　我把一切都给了你们——

里根：　您幸好及时给了我们。

李尔：　叫你们做我的代理人、保管者，我的唯一的条件，只是让我保留这么多的侍从。什么！我只能带二十五个人，到你这儿来吗？里根，你是不是这样说？

里根：　父亲，我可以再说一遍，我只允许您带这么几个人来。

李尔：　恶人的脸相虽然狰狞可怖，要是与比他更恶的人相比，就会显得和蔼可亲；不是绝顶的凶恶，总还有几分可取。（向高纳里尔）我愿意跟你去；你的五十个人还比她的二十五个人多上一倍，你的孝心也比她大一倍。

高纳里尔：　父亲，我们家里难道没有两倍这么多的仆人可以侍候您？依我说，不但用不着二十五个人，就是十个五个也是多余的。

里根：　依我看来，一个也不需要。

KING LEAR.   O, reason not the need! Our basest beggars

    Are in the poorest thing superfluous.

    Allow not nature more than nature needs,

    Man's life is cheap as beast's. Thou art a lady:

    If only to go warm were gorgeous,

    Why, nature needs not what thou gorgeous wear'st

    Which scarcely keeps thee warm. But, for true need –

    You heavens, give me that patience, patience I need!

    You see me here, you gods, a poor old man,

    As full of grief as age; wretched in both.

    If it be you that stirs these daughters' hearts

    Against their father, fool me not so much

    To bear it tamely; touch me with noble anger,

    And let not women's weapons, water drops,

    Stain my man's cheeks! No, you unnatural hags!

    I will have such revenges on you both

    That all the world shall – I will do such things –

    What they are, yet, I know not; but they shall be

    The terrors of the earth! You think I'll weep.

    No, I'll not weep.

    I have full cause of weeping, but this heart

    Shall break into a hundred thousand flaws

    Or ere I'll weep. O fool, I shall go mad!

    [*Exeunt Lear, Gloster, Kent, and Fool.*]

DUKE OF CORNWALL.   Let us withdraw; 'twill be a storm.

李尔：　啊！不要跟我说什么需要不需要；最卑贱的乞丐，也有他的不值钱的身外之物；人生除了天然的需要以外，要是没有其他的享受，那和畜类的生活有什么分别。你是一位夫人；你穿着这样华丽的衣服，如果你的目的只是为了保持温暖，那就根本不合你的需要，因为这种盛装艳饰并不能使你温暖。可是，讲到真的需要，那么天啊，给我忍耐吧，我需要忍耐！神啊，你们看见我在这儿，一个可怜的老头子，被忧伤和老迈折磨得好苦！假如是你们鼓动这两个女儿的心，使她们忤逆她们的父亲，那么请你们不要尽是愚弄我，叫我默然忍受吧；让我的心里激起了刚强的怒火，别让妇人所恃为武器的泪点玷污我的男子汉的面颊！不，你们这两个不孝的妖妇，我要向你们复仇，我要做出一些使全世界惊怖的事情来，虽然我现在还不知道我要怎么做。你们以为我将要哭泣；不，我不愿哭泣，我虽然有充分的哭泣的理由，可是我宁愿让这颗心碎成万片，也不愿流下一滴泪来。啊，傻瓜！我要发疯了！（李尔、葛罗斯特、肯特及弄人同下。）

康华尔：　我们进去吧；一场暴风雨将要来了。（远处暴风雨声。）

REGAN.　This house is little; the old man and 's people

　　Cannot be well bestowed.

GONERIL.　'Tis his own blame; hath put himself from rest

　　And must needs taste his folly.

REGAN.　For his particular, I'll receive him gladly,

　　But not one follower.

GONERIL.　So am I purposed.

　　Where is my Lord of Gloster?

DUKE OF CORNWALL.　Followed the old man forth.

　　[*Enter Gloster.*]

　　He is returned.

EARL OF GLOSTER.　The King is in high rage.

DUKE OF CORNWALL.　Whither is he going?

EARL OF GLOSTER.　He calls to horse, but will I know not whither.

DUKE OF CORNWALL.　'Tis best to give him way; he leads himself.

GONERIL.　My lord, entreat him by no means to stay.

EARL OF GLOSTER.　Alack, the night comes on, and the bleak winds

　　Do sorely ruffle. For many miles about

　　There's scarce a bush.

REGAN.　O, sir, to wilful men

　　The injuries that they themselves procure

　　Must be their schoolmasters. Shut up your doors.

　　He is attended with a desperate train,

　　And what they may incense him to, being apt

　　To have his ear abused, wisdom bids fear.

里根：　这座房屋太小了，这老头儿带着他那班人来是容纳不下的。

高纳里尔：　是他自己不好，放着安逸的日子不过，一定要吃些苦，
　　才知道自己的蠢。

里根：　单是他一个人，我倒也很愿意收留他，可是他的那班跟随
　　的人，我可一个也不能容纳。

高纳里尔：　我也是这个意思。葛罗斯特伯爵呢？

康华尔：　跟老头子出去了。（葛罗斯特重上。）他回来了。

葛罗斯特：　王上正在盛怒之中。

康华尔：　他要到哪儿去？

葛罗斯特：　他叫人备马；可是不让我知道他要到什么地方去。

康华尔：　还是不要管他，随他自己的意思吧。

高纳里尔：　伯爵，您千万不要留他。

葛罗斯特：　唉！天色暗起来了，田野里都在刮着狂风，附近许多
　　里之内，简直连一株小小的树木都没有。

里根：　啊！伯爵，对于刚愎自用的人，只好让他们自己招致的灾
　　祸教训他们。关上您的门；他有一班亡命之徒跟随在身边，他
　　自己又是这样容易受人愚弄，谁也不知道他们会煽动他干出些
　　什么事来。我们还是小心点儿好。

DUKE OF CORNWALL.   Shut up your doors, my lord: 'tis a wild night.

My Regan counsels well. Come out o' th' storm.

[*Exeunt.*]

康华尔：　　关上您的门，伯爵；这是一个狂暴的晚上。我的里根说得一点不错。暴风雨来了，我们进去吧。（同下。）

ACT III   SCENE I

A heath.

[*Storm still. Enter Kent and a Gentleman, severally.*]

EARL OF KENT.   Who's there, besides foul weather?

GENTLEMAN.   One minded like the weather, most unquietly.

EARL OF KENT.   I know you. Where's the King?

GENTLEMAN.   Contending with the fretful elements;

    Bids the wind blow the earth into the sea,

    Or swell the curled waters 'bove the main,

    That things might change or cease; tears his white hair,

    Which the impetuous blasts, with eyeless rage,

    Catch in their fury and make nothing of;

    Strives in his little world of man to out-storm

    The to-and-fro-conflicting wind and rain.

    This night, wherein the cub-drawn bear would couch,

    The lion and the belly-pinched wolf

    Keep their fur dry, unbonneted he runs,

    And bids what will take all.

EARL OF KENT.   But who is with him?

GENTLEMAN.   None but the fool, who labours to out-jest

    His heart-struck injuries.

第三幕　第一场

荒野。

（暴风雨，雷电。肯特及一侍臣上，相遇。）

肯特：　除了恶劣的天气以外，还有谁在这儿？

侍臣：　一个心绪像这天气一样不安静的人。

肯特：　我认识你。王上呢？

侍臣：　正在跟暴怒的大自然竞争；他叫狂风把大地吹下海里，叫泛滥的波涛吞没了陆地，使万物都变了样子或归于毁灭；拉下他的一根根的白发，让挟着盲目的愤怒的暴风把它们卷得不知去向；在他渺小的一身之内，正在进行着一场比暴风雨的冲突更剧烈的斗争。这样的晚上，被小熊吸干了乳汁的母熊，也躲着不敢出来，狮子和饿狼都不愿沾湿它们的毛皮。他却光秃着头在风雨中狂奔，把一切付托给不可知的力量。

肯特：　可是谁和他在一起？

侍臣：　只有那傻瓜一路跟着他，竭力用些笑话替他排解他的心中的伤痛。

EARL OF KENT.　　Sir, I do know you,

　　And dare upon the warrant of my note

　　Commend a dear thing to you. There is division

　　Although as yet the face of it be covered

　　With mutual cunning 'twixt Albany and Cornwall;

　　Who have as who have not, that their great stars

　　Throne and set high? – servants, who seem no less,

　　Which are to France the spies and speculations

　　Intelligent of our state. What hath been seen,

　　Either in snuffs and packings of the Dukes,

　　Or the hard rein which both of them have borne

　　Against the old kind King, or something deeper,

　　Whereof, perchance, these are but furnishings –

　　But, true it is, from France there comes a power

　　Into this scattered kingdom, who already,

　　Wise in our negligence, have secret feet

　　In some of our best ports and are at point

　　To show their open banner. Now to you:

　　If on my credit you dare build so far

　　To make your speed to Dover, you shall find

　　Some that will thank you, making just report

　　Of how unnatural and bemadding sorrow

　　The King hath cause to plain.

　　I am a gentleman of blood and breeding,

　　And from some knowledge and assurance

　　Offer this office to you.

肯特：　我知道你是什么人，我敢凭着我的观察所及，告诉你一件重要的消息。在奥本尼和康华尔两人之间，虽然表面上彼此掩饰得毫无痕迹，可是暗中却已经发生了冲突；正像一般身居高位的人一样，在他们手下都有一些名为仆人、实际上却是向法国密报我们国内情形的探子，凡是这两个公爵的明争暗斗，他们两人对于善良的老王的冷酷的待遇，以及在这种种表象底下，其他更秘密的一切动静，全都传到了法国的耳中；现在已经有一支军队从法国开到我们这一个分裂的国土上来，乘着我们疏忽无备，在我们几处最好的港口秘密登陆，不久就要揭开他们鲜明的旗帜了。现在，你要是能够信任我的话，请你赶快到多佛去一趟，那边你可以碰见有人在欢迎你，你可以把被逼疯了的王上所受种种无理的屈辱向他作一个确实的报告，他一定会感激你的好意。我是一个有地位有身价的绅士，因为知道你的为人可靠，所以把这件差使交给你。

GENTLEMAN.　I will talk further with you.

EARL OF KENT.　No, do not.

> For confirmation that I am much more
>
> Than my out-wall, open this purse and take
>
> What it contains. If you shall see Cordelia
>
> As fear not but you shall, show her this ring,
>
> And she will tell you who your fellow is
>
> That yet you do not know. Fie on this storm!
>
> I will go seek the King.

GENTLEMAN.　Give me your hand. Have you no more to say?

EARL OF KENT.　Few words, but, to effect, more than all yet:

> That, when we have found the King in which your pain
>
> That way, I'll this, he that first lights on him
>
> Holla the other.
>
> [*Exeunt. Severally.*]

侍臣：　　我还要跟您谈谈。

肯特：　　不，不必。为了向你证明我并不是像我的外表那样的一个微贱之人，你可以打开这一个钱囊，把里面的东西拿去。你一到多佛，一定可以见到考狄利娅；只要把这戒指给她看了，她就可以告诉你，你现在所不认识的同伴是个什么人。好可恶的暴风雨！我要找王上去。

侍臣：　　把您的手给我。您没有别的话了吗？

肯特：　　还有一句话，可比什么都重要；就是：我们现在先去找王上；你往那边去，我往这边去，谁先找到他，就打一个招呼。

　　　　　（各下。）

ACT III　SCENE II

Another part of the heath.

[Storm still. Enter Lear and Fool.]

KING LEAR.　Blow, winds, and crack your cheeks! rage! blow!

You cataracts and hurricanoes, spout

Till you have drenched our steeples, drowned the cocks!

You sulphurous and thought-executing fires,

Vaunt-couriers to oak-cleaving thunderbolts,

Singe my white head! And thou, all-shaking thunder,

Strike flat the thick rotundity o' th' world,

Crack Nature's moulds, all germens spill at once,

That makes ingrateful man!

FOOL.　O nuncle, court holy water in a dry house is better than this rain water out o' door. Good nuncle, in, and ask thy daughters blessing! Here's a night pities nether wise men nor fools.

KING LEAR.　Rumble thy bellyful! Spit, fire! spout, rain!

Nor rain, wind, thunder, fire are my daughters.

I tax not you, you elements, with unkindness.

I never gave you kingdom, called you children,

You owe me no subscription. Then let fall

Your horrible pleasure. Here I stand your slave,

第三幕　第二场

荒野的另一部分。

（暴风雨继续未止。李尔和弄人上。）

李尔：　吹吧，风啊！胀破了你的脸颊，猛烈地吹吧！你，瀑布一样的倾盆大雨，尽管倒泻下来，浸没了我们的尖塔，淹沉了屋顶上的风标吧！你，思想一样迅速的硫磺的电火，劈碎橡树的巨雷的先驱，烧焦了我的白发的头颅吧！你，震撼一切的霹雳啊，把这生殖繁密的、饱满的地球击平了吧！打碎造物的模型，不要让一颗忘恩负义的人类的种子遗留在世上！

弄人：　啊，老伯伯，在一间干燥的屋子里说几句好话，不比在这没有遮蔽的旷野里淋雨好得多吗？老伯伯，回到那所房子里去，向你的女儿们请求祝福吧；这样的夜无论对于聪明人或是傻瓜，都是不发一点慈悲的。

李尔：　尽管轰着吧！尽管吐你的火舌，尽管喷你的雨水吧！雨、风、雷、电，都不是我的女儿，我不责怪你们的无情；我不曾给你们国土，不曾称你们为我的孩子，你们没有顺从我的义务；所以，随你们的高兴，降下你们可怕的威力来吧，我站在这儿，只是你们的奴隶，一个可怜的、衰弱的、无力的、遭人贱视的

A poor, infirm, weak, and despised old man.

But yet I call you servile ministers,

That will with two pernicious daughters join

Your high-engendered battles 'gainst a head

So old and white as this! O! O! 'tis foul!

FOOL.　He that has a house to put 's head in has a good head-piece.

The codpiece that will house

Before the head has any,

The head and he shall louse:

So beggars marry many.

The man that makes his toe

What he his heart should make

Shall of a corn cry woe,

And turn his sleep to wake.

for there was never yet fair woman but she made mouths in a glass.

[*Enter Kent.*]

KING LEAR.　No, I will be the pattern of all patience;

I will say nothing.

EARL OF KENT.　Who's there?

FOOL.　Marry, here's grace and a codpiece; that's a wise man and a
fool.

EARL OF KENT.　Alas, sir, are you here? Things that love night

Love not such nights as these. The wrathful skies

老头子。可是我仍然要骂你们是卑劣的帮凶，因为你们滥用上天的威力，帮同两个万恶的女儿来跟我这个白发的老翁作对。啊！啊！这太卑劣了！

弄人：　谁头上顶着个好头脑，就不愁没有屋顶来遮他的头。

脑袋还没找到屋子，
话儿倒先有安乐窝；
脑袋和他都生虱子，
就这么叫花婆老婆。
有人只爱他的脚尖，
不把心儿放在心上；
那鸡眼使他真可怜，
在床上翻身又叫嚷。
从来没有一个美女不是对着镜子做她的鬼脸。

（肯特上。）

李尔：　不，我要忍受众人所不能忍受的痛苦；我要闭口无言。

肯特：　谁在那边？

弄人：　一个是陛下，一个是弄人；这两人一个聪明一个傻。

肯特：　唉！陛下，你在这儿吗？喜爱黑夜的东西，不会喜爱这样的黑夜；狂怒的天色吓怕了黑暗中的漫游者，使它们躲在洞里

Gallow the very wanderers of the dark

And make them keep their caves. Since I was man,

Such sheets of fire, such bursts of horrid thunder,

Such groans of roaring wind and rain, I never

Remember to have heard. Man's nature cannot carry

The affliction nor the fear.

KING LEAR.　　Let the great gods,

That keep this dreadful pother o'er our heads,

Find out their enemies now. Tremble, thou wretch,

That hast within thee undivulged crimes

Unwhipped of justice. Hide thee, thou bloody hand;

Thou perjured, and thou simular man of virtue

That art incestuous. Caitiff, in pieces shake

That under covert and convenient seeming

Hast practised on man's life. Close pent-up guilts,

Rive your concealing continents, and cry

These dreadful summoners grace. I am a man

More sinned against than sinning.

EARL OF KENT.　　Alack, bareheaded?

Gracious my lord, hard by here is a hovel;

Some friendship will it lend you 'gainst the tempest.

Repose you there, whilst I to this hard house

More harder than the stones whereof 'tis raised,

Which even but now, demanding after you,

Denied me to come in return, and force

Their scanted courtesy.

不敢出来。自从有生以来，我从没有看见过这样的闪电，听见过这样可怕的雷声，这样惊人的风雨的咆哮；人类的精神是禁受不起这样的磨折和恐怖的。

李尔：　伟大的神灵在我们头顶掀起这场可怕的骚动。让他们现在找到他们的敌人吧。战栗吧，你尚未被人发觉、逍遥法外的罪人！躲起来吧，你杀人的凶手，你用伪誓欺人的骗子，你道貌岸然的逆伦禽兽！魂飞魄散吧，你用正直的外表遮掩杀人阴谋的大奸巨恶！撕下你们包藏祸心的伪装，显露你们罪恶的原形，向这些可怕的天吏哀号乞命吧！我是个并没有犯多大的罪、却受了很大的冤屈的人。

肯特：　唉！您头上没有一点遮盖的东西！陛下，这儿附近有一间茅屋，可以替您挡挡风雨。我刚才曾经到那所冷酷的屋子里——那比它墙上的石块更冷酷无情的屋子——探问您的行踪，可是他们关上了门不让我进去；现在您且暂时躲一躲雨，我还要回去，非要他们讲一点人情不可。

KING LEAR.　My wits begin to turn.

> Come on, my boy. How dost, my boy? Art cold?
>
> I am cold myself. Where is this straw, my fellow?
>
> The art of our necessities is strange,
>
> That can make vile things precious. Come, your hovel.
>
> Poor fool and knave, I have one part in my heart
>
> That's sorry yet for thee.

FOOL.　[*Sings.*] He that has and a little tiny wit –

> With hey, ho, the wind and the rain –
>
> Must make content with his fortunes fit,
>
> For the rain it raineth every day.

KING LEAR.　True, my good boy. Come, bring us to this hovel.

> [*Exeunt Lear and Kent.*]

FOOL.　This is a brave night to cool a courtesan. I'll speak prophecy a ere I go:

> When priests are more in word than matter;
>
> When brewers mar their malt with water;
>
> When nobles are their tailors' tutors,
>
> No heretics burned, but wenches' suitors;
>
> Then shall the realm of Albion
>
> Come to great confusion.
>
> When every case in law is right,
>
> No squire in debt nor no poor knight;
>
> When slanders do not live in tongues,
>
> Nor cutpurses come not to throngs;

李尔：　　我的头脑开始昏乱起来了。来，我的孩子。你怎么啦，我的孩子？你冷吗？我自己也冷呢。我的朋友，这间茅屋在什么地方？一个人到了困穷无告的时候，微贱的东西竟也会变成无价之宝。来，带我到你那间茅屋里去。可怜的傻小子，我心里还留着一块地方为你悲伤哩。

弄人：　　只怪自己糊涂自己蠢，

　　　　　嗨呵，一阵风来一阵雨，

　　　　　背时倒运莫把天公恨，

　　　　　管它朝朝雨雨又风风。

李尔：　　不错，我的好孩子。来，领我们到这茅屋里去。（李尔、肯特下。）

弄人：　　今天晚上可太凉快了，叫婊子都热不起劲儿来。待我在临走之前，讲几句预言吧：

　　　　　传道的嘴上一味说得好；

　　　　　酿酒的酒里掺水真不少；

　　　　　有钱的大爷教裁缝做活；

　　　　　不烧异教徒；嫖客害流火；

　　　　　若是件件官司都问得清；

　　　　　跟班不欠钱，骑士债还清；

　　　　　世上的是非不出自嘴里；

　　　　　扒儿手看见人堆就躲避；

　　　　　放债的肯让金银露了眼；

　　　　　老鸨和婊子把教堂修建；

When usurers tell their gold i' th' field,

And bawds and whores do churches build:

Then comes the time, who lives to see't,

That going shall be used with feet.

This prophecy Merlin shall make, for I live before his time.

[*Exit.*]

到那时候，英国这个国家，

准会乱得无法收拾一下；

那时活着的都可以看到：

那走路的把脚步抬得高。

其实这番预言该让梅林[1]在将来说，因为我出生在他之前。（下。）

---

1 梅林（Merlin），英格兰传说中亚瑟王的挚友，是术士和预言家。事实上梅林的
 传说要比李尔王晚许多年，这里是作者故意说的笑话。

ACT III   SCENE III

Gloster's Castle.
[*Enter Gloster and Edmund.*]

EARL OF GLOSTER.   Alack, alack, Edmund, I like not this unnatural dealing! When I desired their leave that I might pity him, they took from me the use of mine own house, charged me on pain of perpetual displeasure neither to speak of him, entreat for him, nor any way sustain him.

EDMUND.   Most savage and unnatural!

EARL OF GLOSTER.   Go to; say you nothing. There is division betwixt the Dukes, and a worse matter than that. I have received a letter this night –'tis dangerous to be spoken – I have locked the letter in my closet. These injuries the King now bears will be revenged home; there's part of a power already footed; we must incline to the King. I will seek him and privily relieve him. Go you and maintain talk with the Duke, that my charity be not of him perceived. If he ask for me, I am ill and gone to bed. Though I die for't, as no less is threat'ned me, the King my old master must be relieved. There is some strange thing toward, Edmund. Pray you be careful.

[*Exit.*]

第三幕　第三场

葛罗斯特城堡中的一室。

（葛罗斯特及爱德蒙上。）

葛罗斯特：　唉，唉！爱德蒙，我不赞成这种不近人情的行为。当我请求他们允许我给他一点援助的时候，他们竟会剥夺我使用自己的房屋的权利，不许我提起他的名字，不许我替他说一句恳求的话，也不许我给他任何的救济，要是违背了他们的命令，我就要永远失去他们的欢心。

爱德蒙：　太野蛮、太不近人情了！

葛罗斯特：　算了，你不要多说什么。两个公爵现在已经有了意见，而且还有一件比这更严重的事情。今天晚上我接到一封信，里面的话说出来也是很危险的；我已经把这信锁在壁橱里了。王上受到这样的凌虐，总有人会来替他报复的；已经有一支军队在路上了；我们必须站在王上的一边。我就要找他去，暗地里救济救济他；你去陪公爵谈谈，免得被他觉察了我的行动。要是他问起我，你就回他说我身子不好，已经睡了。大不了是一个死——他们的确拿死来威吓——王上是我的老主人，我不能坐视不救。出人意料之外的事情快要发生了，爱德蒙，你必须小心点儿。（下。）

EDMUND.　This courtesy, forbid thee, shall the Duke

 Instantly know, and of that letter too.

 This seems a fair deserving, and must draw me

 That which my father loses – no less than all.

 The younger rises when the old doth fall.

 [*Exit.*]

爱德蒙：　　你违背了命令去献这种殷勤，我立刻就要去告诉公爵知道；还有那封信我也要告诉他。这是我献功邀赏的好机会，我的父亲将要因此而丧失他所有的一切，也许他的全部家产都要落到我的手里；老的一代没落了，年轻的一代才会兴起。（下。）

ACT III   SCENE IV

The heath. Before a hovel.

[Enter Lear, Kent, and Fool.]

EARL OF KENT.   Here is the place, my lord. Good my lord, enter.

    The tyranny of the open night 's too rough

    For nature to endure. *[Storm still.]*

KING LEAR.   Let me alone.

EARL OF KENT.   Good my lord, enter here.

KING LEAR.   Wilt break my heart?

EARL OF KENT.   I had rather break mine own. Good my lord, enter.

KING LEAR.   Thou think'st 'tis much that this contentious storm

    Invades us to the skin. So 'tis to thee;

    But where the greater malady is fixed,

    The lesser is scarce felt. Thouedst shun a bear;

    But if thy flight lay toward the raging sea,

    Thouedst meet the bear i' th' mouth. When the mind's free,

    The body's delicate. The tempest in my mind

    Doth from my senses take all feeling else

    Save what beats there. Filial ingratitude!

    Is it not as this mouth should tear this hand

    For lifting food to't? But I will punish home!

第三幕　第四场

荒野。茅屋之前。

（李尔、肯特及弄人上。）

肯特：　就是这地方，陛下，进去吧。在这样毫无掩庇的黑夜里，像这样的狂风暴雨，谁也受不了的。（暴风雨继续不止。）

李尔：　不要缠着我。

肯特：　陛下，进去吧。

李尔：　你要碎裂我的心吗？

肯特：　我宁愿碎裂我自己的心。陛下，进去吧。

李尔：　你以为让这样的狂风暴雨侵袭我们的肌肤，是一件了不得的苦事；在你看来是这样的；可是一个人要是身染重病，他就不会感觉到小小的痛楚。你见了一头熊就要转身逃走；可是假如你的背后是汹涌的大海，你就只好硬着头皮向那头熊迎面走去了。当我们心绪宁静的时候，我们的肉体才是敏感的；我的心灵中的暴风雨已经取去我一切其他的感觉，只剩下心头的热血在那儿搏动。儿女的忘恩！这不就像这一只手把食物送进这一张嘴里，这一张嘴却把这一只手咬了下来吗？可是我要重重惩罚她们。不，我不愿再哭泣了。在这样的夜里，把我关在门外！尽管倒下来吧，什么大雨我都可以忍受。在这样的一个夜里！啊，里根，高纳里尔！你们年老仁慈的父亲一片诚心，把

No, I will weep no more. In such a night

To shut me out! Pour on; I will endure.

In such a night as this! O Regan, Goneril!

Your old kind father, whose frank heart gave all!

O, that way madness lies; let me shun that!

No more of that.

EARL OF KENT.   Good my lord, enter here.

KING LEAR.   Prithee go in thyself; seek thine own ease.

This tempest will not give me leave to ponder

On things would hurt me more. But I'll go in.

[*To the Fool.*] In, boy; go first. – You houseless poverty

Nay, get thee in. I'll pray, and then I'll sleep.

[*Fool goes in.*]

Poor naked wretches, wheresoe'er you are,

That bide the pelting of this pitiless storm,

How shall your houseless heads and unfed sides,

Your looped and windowed raggedness, defend you

From seasons such as these? O, I have ta'en

Too little care of this! Take physic, pomp;

Expose thyself to feel what wretches feel,

That thou mayst shake the superflux to them

And show the heavens more just.

EDGAR.   [*Within.*] Fathom and half, fathom and half!

Poor Tom!

[*The Fool runs out from the hovel.*]

一切都给了你们——啊！那样想下去是要发疯的；我不要想起那些；别再提起那些话了。

肯特：　　陛下，进去吧。

李尔：　　请你自己进去，找一个躲身的地方吧。这暴风雨不肯让我仔细思想种种的事情，那些事情我越想下去，越会增加我的痛苦。可是我要进去。（向弄人）进去，孩子，你先走。你们这些无家可归的人——你进去吧。我要祈祷，然后我要睡一会儿。

（弄人入内。）衣不蔽体的不幸的人们，无论你们在什么地方，都得忍受着这样无情的暴风雨的袭击，你们的头上没有片瓦遮身，你们的腹中饥肠雷动，你们的衣服千疮百孔，怎么抵挡得了这样的气候呢？啊！我一向太没有想到这种事情了。安享荣华的人们啊，睁开你们的眼睛来，到外面来体味一下穷人所忍受的苦，分一些你们享用不了的福泽给他们，让上天知道你们不是全无心肝的人吧！

爱德伽：　　（在内）九英尺深，九英尺深！可怜的汤姆！

（弄人自屋内奔出。）

FOOL.　Come not in here, nuncle, here's a spirit. Help me, help me!

EARL OF KENT.　Give me thy hand. Who's there?

FOOL.　A spirit, a spirit! He says his name's poor Tom.

EARL OF KENT.　What art thou that dost grumble there i' th' straw?
　　Come forth.

[*Enter Edgar disguised as a madman.*]

EDGAR.　Away! the foul fiend follows me!
　　Through the sharp hawthorn blows the cold wind.
　　Hum! go to thy cold bed, and warm thee.

KING LEAR.　Hast thou given all to thy two daughters,
　　And art thou come to this?

EDGAR.　Who gives anything to poor Tom? whom the foul fiend hath
　　led through fire and through flame, through ford and whirlpool,
　　o'er bog and quagmire; that hath laid knives under his pillow and
　　halters in his pew, set ratsbane by his porridge, made him proud of
　　heart, to ride on a bay trotting horse over four-inched bridges, to
　　course his own shadow for a traitor. Bless thy five wits! Tom 's
　　acold. O, do de, do de, do de. Bless thee from whirlwinds,
　　star-blasting, and taking! Do poor Tom some charity, whom the
　　foul fiend vexes. There could I have him now – and there – and
　　there again – and there!
　　[*Storm still.*]

KING LEAR.　What, have his daughters brought him to this pass?

弄人：　　老伯伯，不要进去；里面有一个鬼。救命！救命！

肯特：　　让我搀着你，谁在里边？

弄人：　　一个鬼，一个鬼；他说他的名字叫做可怜的汤姆。

肯特：　　你是什么人，在这茅屋里大呼小叫的？出来。

（爱德伽乔装疯人上。）

爱德伽：　　走开！恶魔跟在我的背后！"风儿吹过山楂林。"哼！
　　　　　　到你冷冰冰的床上暖一暖你的身体吧。

李尔：　　你把你所有的一切都给了你的两个女儿，所以才到今天这
　　　　　地步吗？

爱德伽：　　谁把什么东西给可怜的汤姆？恶魔带着他穿过大火，穿
　　　　　　过烈焰，穿过水道和漩涡，穿过沼地和泥泞；把刀子放在他的
　　　　　　枕头底下，把绳子放在他的凳子底下，把毒药放在他的粥里；
　　　　　　使他心中骄傲，骑了一匹栗色的奔马，从四英寸阔的桥梁上过
　　　　　　去，把他自己的影子当做了一个叛徒，紧紧追逐不舍。祝福你
　　　　　　的五种才智！汤姆冷着呢。啊！哆啼哆啼哆啼。愿旋风不吹你，
　　　　　　星星不把毒箭射你，瘟疫不到你身上！做做好事，救救那给恶
　　　　　　魔害得好苦的可怜的汤姆吧！他现在就在那儿，在那儿，又到
　　　　　　那儿去了，在那儿。（暴风雨继续不止。）

李尔：　　什么！他的女儿害得他变成这个样子吗？你不能留下一些

Couldst thou save nothing? Didst thou give 'em all?

FOOL.   Nay, he reserved a blanket, else we had been all shamed.

KING LEAR.   Now all the plagues that in the pendulous air

Hang fated o'er men's faults light on thy daughters!

EARL OF KENT.   He hath no daughters, sir.

KING LEAR.   Death, traitor! nothing could have subdued nature

To such a lowness but his unkind daughters.

Is it the fashion that discarded fathers

Should have thus little mercy on their flesh?

Judicious punishment! 'Twas this flesh begot

Those pelican daughters.

EDGAR.   Pillicock sat on Pillicock Hill. 'Alow,

'alow, loo, loo!

FOOL.   This cold night will turn us all to fools and madmen.

EDGAR.   Take heed o' th' foul fiend; obey thy parents: keep thy word
justly; swear not; commit not with man's sworn spouse; set not thy
sweet heart on proud array. Tom 's acold.

KING LEAR.   What hast thou been?

EDGAR.   A serving-man, proud in heart and mind; that curled my hair,
wore gloves in my cap; served the lust of my mistress' heart and
did the act of darkness with her; swore as many oaths as I spake
words, and broke them in the sweet face of heaven; one that slept
in the ontriving of lust, and waked to do it. Wine loved I deeply,
dice dearly; and in woman out-paramoured the Turk. False of
heart, light of ear, bloody of hand; hog in sloth, fox in stealth, wolf
in greediness, dog in madness, lion in prey. Let not the creaking

什么来吗？你一起都给了她们了吗？

弄人：　不，他还留着一方毡毯，否则我们大家都要不好意思了。

李尔：　愿那弥漫在天空之中的惩罚恶人的瘟疫一起降临在你的女儿身上！

肯特：　陛下，他没有女儿哩。

李尔：　该死的奸贼！他没有不孝的女儿，怎么会流落到这等不堪的地步？难道被弃的父亲，都是这样一点不爱惜他们自己的身体的吗？适当的处罚！谁叫他们的身体产下那些枭獍般的女儿来？

爱德伽：　"小雄鸡坐在高墩上，"呵罗，呵罗，罗，罗！

弄人：　这一个寒冷的夜晚将要使我们大家变成傻瓜和疯子。

爱德伽：　当心恶魔。孝顺你的爷娘；说过的话不要反悔；不要赌咒；不要奸淫有夫之妇；不要把你的情人打扮得太漂亮。汤姆冷着呢。

李尔：　你本来是干什么的？

爱德伽：　一个心性高傲的仆人，头发卷得曲曲的，帽子上佩着情人的手套，惯会讨妇女的欢心，干些不可告人的勾当；开口发誓，闭口赌咒，当着上天的面前把它们一个个毁弃，睡梦里都在转奸淫的念头，一醒来便把它实行。我贪酒，我爱赌，我比土耳其人更好色；一颗奸诈的心，一对轻信的耳朵，一双不怕血腥气的手；猪一般懒惰，狐狸一般狡诡，狼一般贪狠，狗一般疯狂，狮子一般凶恶。不要让女人的脚步声和窸窸窣窣的绸衣裳的声音摄去了你的魂魄；不要把你的脚踏进窑子里去；不

of shoes nor the rustling of silks betray thy poor heart to woman. Keep thy foot out of brothel, thy hand out of placket, thy pen from lender's book, and defy the foul fiend. Still through the hawthorn blows the cold wind; Says suum, mun, hey, no, nonny. Dolphin my boy, my boy, sessa! Let him trot by.

[*Storm still.*]

KING LEAR.   Why, thou wert better in thy grave than to answer with thy uncovered body this extremity of the skies. Is man no more than this? Consider him well. Thou ow'st the worm no silk, the beast no hide, the sheep no wool, the cat no perfume. Ha! Here's three on's are sophisticated! Thou art the thing itself; unaccommodated man is no more but such a poor, bare, forked animal as thou art. Off, off, you lendings! Come, unbutton here.

[*Tears at his clothes.*]

FOOL.   Prithee, nuncle, be contented! 'Tis a naughty night to swim in.

[*Enter Gloster with a torch.*]

Now a little fire in a wild field were like an old lecher's heart – a small spark, all the rest on's body cold. Look, here comes a walking fire.

EDGAR.   This is the foul fiend Flibbertigibbet. He begins at curfew, and walks till the first cock. He gives the web and the pin, squints the eye, and makes the harelip; mildews the white wheat, and hurts the poor creature of earth.

Swithold footed thrice the 'old;

He met the nightmare, and her nine fold;

要把你的手伸进裙子里去；不要把你的笔碰到放债人的账簿上；抵抗恶魔的引诱吧。"冷风还是打山楂树里吹过去"；听它怎么说，吁——吁——呜——呜——哈——哈——。道芬我的孩子，我的孩子；叱嚓！让他奔过去。（暴风雨继续不止。）

李尔：　唉，你这样赤身裸体，受风雨的吹淋，还是死了的好。难道人不过是这样一个东西吗？想一想他吧。你也不向蚕身上借一根丝，也不向野兽身上借一张皮，也不向羊身上借一片毛，也不向麝猫身上借一块香料。嗨！我们这三个人都已经失掉了本来的面目，只有你才保全着天赋的原形；人类在草昧的时代，不过是像你这样的一个寒碜的赤裸的两脚动物。脱下来，脱下来，你们这些身外之物！来，松开你的纽扣。（扯去衣服。）

弄人：　老伯伯，请你安静点儿！这样危险的夜里是不能游泳的。（葛罗斯特持火炬上。）旷野里一点小小的火光，正像一个好色的老头儿的心，只有这么一星星的热，他的全身都是冰冷的。瞧！一团火走来了。

爱德伽：　这就是那个叫做"弗力勃铁捷贝特"的恶魔；他在黄昏的时候出现，一直到第一声鸡啼方才隐去；他叫人眼睛里长白膜，叫好眼变成斜眼；他叫人嘴唇上起裂缝；他还会叫面粉发霉，寻穷人们的开心。

　　　　　　圣维都尔三次经过山岗，
　　　　　　遇见魇魔和她九个儿郎；

Bid her alight

And her troth plight,

And aroint thee, witch, aroint thee!

EARL OF KENT.   How fares your Grace?

KING LEAR.   What's he?

EARL OF KENT.   Who's there? What is't you seek?

EARL OF GLOSTER.   What are you there? Your names?

EDGAR.   Poor Tom, that eats the swimming frog, the toad, the tadpole,
the wall-newt and the water; that in the fury of his heart, when the
foul fiend rages, eats cow-dung for sallets, swallows the old rat and
the ditch-dog, drinks the green mantle of the standing pool; who is
whipped from tithing to tithing, and stock-punished and imprisoned;
who hath had three suits to his back, six shirts to his body, Horse to
ride, and weapons to wear; But mice and rats, and such small deer,
Have been Tom's food for seven long year. Beware my follower.
Peace, Smulkin! peace, thou fiend!

EARL OF GLOSTER.   What, hath your Grace no better company?

EDGAR.   The prince of darkness is a gentleman! Modo he's called,
and Mahu.

EARL OF GLOSTER.   Our flesh and blood is grown so vile, my lord,
That it doth hate what gets it.

EDGAR.   Poor Tom 's acold.

EARL OF GLOSTER.   Go in with me. My duty cannot suffer
T' obey in all your daughters' hard commands.
Though their injunction be to bar my doors
And let this tyrannous night take hold upon you,

　　　　　　他说妖精快下马，

　　　　　　发过誓儿快逃吧；

　　　　　　去你的，妖精，去你的！

肯特：　　陛下，您怎么啦？

李尔：　　他是谁？

肯特：　　那儿什么人？你找谁？

葛罗斯特：　你们是些什么人？你们叫什么名字？

爱德伽：　可怜的汤姆，他吃的是泅水的青蛙、蛤蟆、蝌蚪、壁虎
　　　　和水蜥；恶魔在他心里捣乱的时候，他发起狂来，就会把牛粪
　　　　当做一盆美味的生菜；他吞的是老鼠和死狗，喝的是一潭死水
　　　　上面绿色的浮渣；他到处给人家鞭打，锁在枷里，关在牢里；
　　　　他从前有三身外衣、六件衬衫，跨着一匹马，带着一口剑；可
　　　　是在这整整七年时光，耗子是汤姆唯一的食粮。留心那跟在我
　　　　背后的鬼。不要闹，史墨金！不要闹，你这恶魔！

葛罗斯特：　什么！陛下竟会跟这种人作起伴来了吗？

爱德伽：　地狱里的魔王是一个绅士；他的名字叫做摩陀，又叫做
　　　　玛呼。

葛罗斯特：　陛下，我们亲生的骨肉都变得那样坏，把自己生身之
　　　　人当做了仇敌。

爱德伽：　可怜的汤姆冷着呢。

葛罗斯特：　跟我回去吧。我的良心不允许我全然服从您的女儿的
　　　　无情的命令；虽然他们叫我关上了门，把您丢下在这狂暴的黑
　　　　夜之中，可是我还是大胆出来找您，把您带到有火炉、有食物
　　　　的地方去。

Yet have I ventured to come seek you out

And bring you where both fire and food is ready.

KING LEAR.　　First let me talk with this philosopher.

What is the cause of thunder?

EARL OF KENT.　　Good my lord, take his offer; go into th' house.

KING LEAR.　　I'll talk a word with this same learned Theban.

What is your study?

EDGAR.　　How to prevent the fiend and to kill vermin.

KING LEAR.　　Let me ask you one word in private.

EARL OF KENT.　　Importune him once more to go, my lord. His wits

begin t' unsettle.

[*Storm still.*]

EARL OF GLOSTER.　　Canst thou blame him?

His daughters seek his death. Ah, that good Kent!

He said it would be thus – poor banished man!

Thou say'st the King grows mad: I'll tell thee, friend,

I am almost mad myself. I had a son,

Now outlawed from my blood. He sought my life

But lately, very late. I loved him, friend –

No father his son dearer. True to tell thee,

[*Storm still.*]

The grief hath crazed my wits. What a night 's this!

I do beseech your Grace –

KING LEAR.　　O, cry you mercy, sir.

李尔：　　让我先跟这位哲学家谈谈。天上打雷是什么缘故？

肯特：　　陛下，接受他的好意；跟他回去吧。

李尔：　　我还要跟这位学者说一句话。您研究的是哪一门学问？

爱德伽：　　抵御恶魔的战略和消灭毒虫的方法。

李尔：　　让我私下里问您一句话。

肯特：　　大人，请您再催催他吧；他的神经有点儿错乱起来了。

（暴风雨继续不止。）

葛罗斯特：　　你能怪他吗？他的女儿要他死哩。唉！那善良的肯特，他早就说过会有这么一天的，可怜的被放逐的人！你说王上要疯了；告诉你吧，朋友，我自己也差不多疯了。我有一个儿子，现在我已经跟他断绝关系了；他要谋害我的生命，这还是最近的事；我爱他，朋友，没有一个父亲比我更爱他的儿子；不瞒你说，（暴风雨继续不止）我的头脑都气昏了。这是一个什么晚上！陛下，求求您——

李尔：　　啊！请您原谅，先生。高贵的哲学家，请了。

Noble philosopher, your company.

EDGAR.　　Tom's acold.

EARL OF GLOSTER.　　In, fellow, there, into th' hovel; keep thee warm.

KING LEAR.　　Come, let's in all.

EARL OF KENT.　　This way, my lord.

KING LEAR.　　With him!

I will keep still with my philosopher.

EARL OF KENT.　　Good my lord, soothe him; let him take the fellow.

EARL OF GLOSTER.　　Take him you on.

EARL OF KENT.　　Sirrah, come on; go along with us.

KING LEAR.　　Come, good Athenian.

EARL OF GLOSTER.　　No words, no words! hush.

EDGAR.　　Child Rowland to the dark tower came;

His word was still Fie, foh, and fum!

I smell the blood of a British man.

[*Exeunt.*]

爱德伽： 汤姆冷着呢。

葛罗斯特： 进去，家伙，到这茅屋里去暖一暖吧。

李尔： 来，我们大家进去。

肯特： 陛下，这边走。

李尔： 带着他；我要跟我这位哲学家在一起。

肯特： 大人，顺顺他的意思吧；让他把这家伙带去。

葛罗斯特： 您带着他来吧。

肯特： 小子，来；跟我们一块儿去。

李尔： 来，好雅典人。

葛罗斯特： 嘘！不要说话，不要说话。

爱德伽： 罗兰骑士来到黑沉沉的古堡前，他说了一遍又一遍："呸，嘿，哼！"我闻到了一股不列颠人的血腥。（同下。）

ACT III   SCENE V

Gloster's Castle.
[*Enter Cornwall and Edmund.*]

DUKE OF CORNWALL.   I will have my revenge ere I depart his house.

EDMUND.   How, my lord, I may be censured, that nature thus gives way to loyalty, something fears me to think of.

DUKE OF CORNWALL.   I now perceive it was not altogether your brother's evil disposition made him seek his death; but a provoking merit, set a-work by a reprovable badness in himself.

EDMUND.   How malicious is my fortune that I must repent t be just! This is the letter he spoke of, which approves him an intelligent party to th advantages of France. O heavens! That this treason were not – or not I the detector!

DUKE OF CORNWALL.   Go with me to the Duchess.

EDMUND.   If the matter of this paper be certain, you have mighty business in hand.

DUKE OF CORNWALL.   True or false, it hath made thee Earl of Gloster. Seek out where thy father is, that he may be ready for our apprehension.

EDMUND.   [*Aside.*] If I find him comforting the King, it will stuff his suspicion more fully. – I will persever in my course of loyalty,

第三幕　第五场

葛罗斯特城堡中一室。

（康华尔及爱德蒙上。）

康华尔：　我在离开他的屋子以前，一定要把他惩治一下。

爱德蒙：　殿下，我为了尽忠的缘故，不顾父子之情，一想到人家不知将要怎样批评我，心里很有点儿惴惴不安哩。

康华尔：　我现在才知道你的哥哥想要谋害他的生命，并不完全出于恶毒的本性；多半是他自己咎有应得，才会引起他的杀心的。

爱德蒙：　我的命运多么颠倒，虽然做了正义的事情，却必须抱恨终身！这就是他说起的那封信，它可以证实他私通法国的罪状。天啊！为什么他要干这种叛逆的行为，为什么偏偏又在我手里发觉了呢？

康华尔：　跟我见公爵夫人去。

爱德蒙：　这信上所说的事情倘然属实，那您就要有一番重大的行动了。

康华尔：　不管它是真是假，它已经使你成为葛罗斯特伯爵了。你去找找你父亲在什么地方，让我们可以把他逮捕起来。

爱德蒙：　（旁白）要是我看见他正在援助那老王，他的嫌疑就格外加重了。——虽然忠心和孝道在我的灵魂里发生剧烈的争战，

though the conflict be sore between that and my blood.

DUKE OF CORNWALL.   I will lay trust upon thee, and thou shalt find a dearer father in my love.

[*Exeunt.*]

可是大义所在，只好把私恩抛弃不顾。

康华尔： 我完全信任你；你在我的恩宠之中，将要得到一个更慈
　　　　爱的父亲。（各下。）

ACT III   SCENE VI

A farmhouse near Gloster's Castle.
[*Enter Gloster, Lear, Kent, Fool, and Edgar.*]

EARL OF GLOSTER.   Here is better than the open air; take it thankfully. I will piece out the comfort with what addition I can. I will not be long from you.

EARL OF KENT.   All the power of his wits have given way to his impatience. The gods reward your kindness!

[*Exit Gloster.*]

EDGAR.   Frateretto calls me, and tells me Nero is an angler in the lake of darkness. Pray, innocent, and beware the foul fiend.

FOOL.   Prithee, nuncle, tell me whether a madman be a gentleman or a yeoman.

KING LEAR.   A king, a king!

FOOL.   No, he's a yeoman that has a gentleman to his son; for he's a mad yeoman that sees his son a gentleman before him.

KING LEAR.   To have a thousand with red burning spits
    Come hissing in upon 'em –

EDGAR.   The foul fiend bites my back.

FOOL.   He's mad that trusts in the tameness of a wolf, a horse's health, a boy's love, or a whore's oath.

第三幕　第六场

邻接城堡的农舍一室。

（葛罗斯特、李尔、肯特、弄人及爱德伽上。）

葛罗斯特：　这儿比露天好一些，不要嫌它寒碜，将就住下来吧。
　　　　我再去找找有些什么吃的用的东西；我去去就来。

肯特：　他的智力已经在他的盛怒之中完全消失了。神明报答您的
　　　　好心！（葛罗斯特下。）

爱德伽：　弗拉特累多在叫我，他告诉我尼禄王在冥湖里钓鱼。喂，
　　　　傻瓜，你要祷告，要留心恶魔啊。

弄人：　老伯伯，告诉我，一个疯子是绅士呢还是平民？

李尔：　是个国王，是个国王！

弄人：　不，他是一个平民，他的儿子却挣了一个绅士头衔；他眼
　　　　看他儿子做了绅士，他就成为一个气疯了的平民。

李尔：　一千条血红的火舌吱啦吱啦卷到她们的身上——

爱德伽：　恶魔在咬我的背。

弄人：　谁要是相信豺狼的驯良、马儿的健康、孩子的爱情或是娼
　　　　妓的盟誓，他就是个疯子。

KING LEAR.　It shall be done; I will arraign them straight.

[*To Edgar.*] Come, sit thou here, most learned ned justicer.

[*To the Fool.*] Thou, sapient sir, sit here. Now, you she-foxes!

EDGAR.　Look, where he stands and glares! Want'st thou eyes at trial, madam? Come o'er the bourn, Bessy, to me.

FOOL.　Her boat hath a leak,

And she must not speak

Why she dares not come over to thee.

EDGAR.　The foul fiend haunts poor Tom in the voice of a nightingale. Hopdance cries in Tom's belly for two white herring. Croak not, black angel; I have no food for thee.

EARL OF KENT.　How do you, sir? Stand you not so amazed. Will you lie down and rest upon the cushions?

KING LEAR.　I'll see their trial first. Bring in their evidence.

[*To Edgar.*] Thou, robed man of justice, take thy place.

[*To the Fool.*] And thou, his yokefellow of equity, Bench by his side.

[*To Kent.*] You are o' th' commission, Sit you too.

EDGAR.　Let us deal justly.

Sleepest or wakest thou, jolly shepherd?

Thy sheep be in the corn;

And for one blast of thy minikin mouth

Thy sheep shall take no harm.

Purr! the cat is gray.

KING LEAR.　Arraign her first. 'Tis Goneril. I here take my oath before this honourable assembly, she kicked the poor King her father.

李尔：　一定要办她们一办，我现在就要审问她们。（向爱德伽）来，最有学问的法官，你坐在这儿；（向弄人）你，贤明的官长，坐在这儿。——来，你们这两头雌狐！

爱德伽：　瞧，他站在那儿，眼睛睁得大大的！太太，你在审判的时候，要不要有人瞧着你？渡过河来会我，蓓西——

弄人：　她的小船儿漏了，

她不能让你知道

为什么她不敢见你。

爱德伽：　恶魔借着夜莺的喉咙，向可怜的汤姆作祟了。霍普丹斯在汤姆的肚子里嚷着要两条新鲜的鲱鱼。别吵，魔鬼；我没有东西给你吃。

肯特：　陛下，您怎么啦！不要这样呆呆地站着。您愿意躺下来，在这褥垫上面休息休息吗？

李尔：　我要先看她们受了审判再说。把她们的证人带上来。（向爱德伽）你这披着法衣的审判官，请坐；（向弄人）你，他的执法的同僚，坐在他的旁边。（向肯特）你是陪审官，你也坐下。

爱德伽：　让我们秉公裁判。

你睡着还是醒着，牧羊人？

你的羊儿在田里跑；

你的小嘴唇只要吹一声，

羊儿就不伤一根毛。

呼噜呼噜；这是一只灰色的猫儿。

李尔：　先控诉她；她是高纳里尔。我当着尊严的堂上起誓，她曾经踢她的可怜的父王。

FOOL.　Come hither, mistress. Is your name Goneril?

KING LEAR.　She cannot deny it.

FOOL.　Cry you mercy, I took you for a joint-stool.

KING LEAR.　And here's another, whose warped looks proclaim

What store her heart is made on. Stop her there!

Arms, arms! sword! fire!

Corruption in the place!

False justicer, why hast thou let her scape?

EDGAR.　Bless thy five wits!

EARL OF KENT.　O pity! Sir, where is the patience now

That you so oft have boasted to retain?

EDGAR.　[*Aside.*] My tears begin to take his part so much

They'll mar my counterfeiting.

KING LEAR.　The little dogs and all,

Tray, Blanch, and Sweetheart, see, they bark at me.

EDGAR.　Tom will throw his head at them. Avaunt, you curs!

Be thy mouth or black or white,

Tooth that poisons if it bite;

Mastiff, greyhound, mongrel grim,

Hound or spaniel, brach or lym,

Bobtail tyke or trundle-tall-

Tom will make them weep and wail;

For, with throwing thus my head,

Dogs leap the hatch, and all are fled.

Do de, de, de. Sessa! Come, march to wakes and fairs and market

towns. Poor Tom, thy horn is dry.

弄人： 过来，奶奶。你的名字叫高纳里尔吗？

李尔： 她不能抵赖。

弄人： 对不起，我还以为您是一张折凳哩。

李尔： 这儿还有一个，你们瞧她满脸的横肉，就可以知道她的心肠是怎么样的。拦住她！举起你们的兵器，拔出你们的剑，点起火把来！营私舞弊的法庭！枉法的贪官，你为什么放她逃走？

爱德伽： 天保佑你的神志吧！

肯特： 哎哟！陛下，您不是常常说您没有失去忍耐吗？现在您的忍耐呢？

爱德伽： （旁白）我的滚滚的热泪忍不住为他流下，怕要给他们瞧破我的假装了。

李尔： 这些小狗：脱雷、勃尔趋、史威塔，瞧，它们都在向我狂吠。

爱德伽： 让汤姆掉过脸来把它们吓走。滚开，你们这些恶狗！

黑嘴巴，白嘴巴，

疯狗咬人磨毒牙，

猛犬猎犬杂种犬，

叭儿小犬团团转，

青屁股，卷尾毛，

汤姆一只也不饶；

只要我掉过脸来，

大狗小狗逃得快。

哆啼哆啼。叱嚓！来，我们赶庙会，上市集去。可怜的汤姆，你的牛角里干得挤不出一滴水来啦。

KING LEAR.　Then let them anatomize Regan. See what breeds about her heart. Is there any cause in nature that makes these hard hearts? [*To Edgar.*] You, sir – I entertain you for one of my hundred; only I do not like the fashion of your garments. You'll say they are Persian attire; but let them be changed.

EARL OF KENT.　Now, good my lord, lie here and rest awhile.

KING LEAR.　Make no noise, make no noise; draw the curtains. So, so, so. We'll go to supper i' th' morning. So, so, so.

FOOL.　And I'll go to bed at noon.

[*Enter Gloster.*]

EARL OF GLOSTER.　Come hither, friend. Where is the King my master?

EARL OF KENT.　Here, sir; but trouble him not; his wits are gone.

EARL OF GLOSTER.　Good friend, I prithee take him in thy arms.

I have o'erheard a plot of death upon him.

There is a litter ready; lay him in't

And drive towards Dover, friend, where thou shalt meet

Both welcome and protection. Take up thy master.

If thou shouldst dally half an hour, his life,

With thine, and all that offer to defend him,

Stand in assured loss. Take up, take up!

And follow me, that will to some provision

Give thee quick conduct.

李尔：　叫他们剖开里根的身体来，看看她心里有些什么东西。究竟为了什么天然的原因，她们的心才会变得这样硬？（向爱德伽）我把你收留下来，叫你做我一百名侍卫中间的一个，只是我不喜欢你的衣服的式样；你也许要对我说，这是最漂亮的波斯装；可是我看还是请你换一换吧。

肯特：　陛下，您还是躺下来休息休息吧。

李尔：　不要吵，不要吵；放下帐子，好，好，好。我们到早上再去吃晚饭吧；好，好，好。

弄人：　我一到中午可要睡觉哩。

（葛罗斯特重上。）

葛罗斯特：　过来，朋友；王上呢？

肯特：　在这儿，大人；可是不要打扰他，他的神经已经错乱了。

葛罗斯特：　好朋友，请你把他抱起来。我已经听到了一个谋害他生命的阴谋。马车套好在外边，你快把他放进去，驾着它到多佛，那边有人会欢迎你，并且会保障你的安全。抱起你的主人来；要是你耽误了半点钟的时间，他的性命、你的性命以及一切出力救护他的人的性命，都要保不住了。抱起来，抱起来；跟我来，让我设法把你们赶快送到一处可以安身的地方。

EARL OF KENT.   Oppressed nature sleeps.

This rest might yet have balmed thy broken senses,

Which, if convenience will not allow,

Stand in hard cure.

[*To the Fool.*] Come, help to bear thy master.

Thou must not stay behind.

EARL OF GLOSTER.   Come, come, away!

[*Exeunt Kent, Gloster, and the Fool, bearing off Lear.*]

EDGAR.   When we our betters see bearing our woes,

We scarcely think our miseries our foes.

Who alone suffers suffers most i' th' mind,

Leaving free things and happy shows behind;

But then the mind much sufferance doth o'erskip

When grief hath mates, and bearing fellowship.

How light and portable my pain seems now,

When that which makes me bend makes the King bow,

He childed as I fathered! Tom, away!

Mark the high noises, and thyself bewray

When false opinion, whose wrong thought defiles thee,

In thy just proof repeals and reconciles thee.

What will hap more to-night, safe scape the King!Lurk,

[*Exit.*]

肯特：　受尽折磨的身心，现在安然入睡了；安息也许可以镇定镇定他的破碎的神经，但愿上天行个方便，不要让它破碎得不可收拾才好。（向弄人）来，帮我抬起你的主人来；你也不能留在这儿。

葛罗斯特：　来，来，去吧。

　　（除爱德伽外，肯特、葛罗斯特及弄人舁李尔下。）

爱德伽：　　做君王的不免如此下场，
　　　　　　使我忘却了自己的忧伤。
　　　　　　最大的不幸是独抱牢愁，
　　　　　　任何的欢娱兜不上心头；
　　　　　　倘有了同病相怜的侣伴，
　　　　　　天大痛苦也会解去一半。
　　　　　　国王有的是不孝的逆女，
　　　　　　我自己遭逢无情的严父，
　　　　　　他与我两个人一般遭际！
　　　　　　去吧，汤姆，忍住你的怨气，
　　　　　　你现在蒙着无辜的污名，
　　　　　　总有日回复你清白之身。
　　　　　　不管今夜里还会发生些什么事情，但愿王上能安然出险！我还是躲起来吧。（下。）

ACT III SCENE VII

Gloster's Castle.

[Enter Cornwall, Regan, Goneril, Edmund the Bastard, and Servants.]

DUKE OF CORNWALL. *[To Goneril.]* Post speedily to my lord your
husband, show him this letter. The army of France is landed. – Seek
out the traitor Gloster. *[Exeunt some of the Servants.]*

REGAN. Hang him instantly.

GONERIL. Pluck out his eyes.

DUKE OF CORNWALL. Leave him to my displeasure. Edmund,
keep you our sister company. The revenges we are bound to take
upon your traitorous father are not fit for your beholding. Advise
the Duke where you are going, to a most festinate preparation. We
are bound to the like. Our posts shall be swift and intelligent
betwixt us. Farewell, dear sister; farewell, my Lord of Gloster.

[Enter Oswald the Steward.]

DUKE OF CORNWALL. How now? Where's the King?

OSWALD. My Lord of Gloster hath conveyed him hence.
Some five or six and thirty of his knights,
Hot questrists after him, met him at gate;

第三幕　第七场

葛罗斯特城堡中一室。

（康华尔、里根、高纳里尔、爱德蒙及众仆上。）

康华尔：　（向高纳里尔）夫人，请您赶快到尊夫的地方去，把这封信交给他；法国军队已经登陆了。——来人，替我去搜寻那反贼葛罗斯特的踪迹。（若干仆人下。）

里根：　把他捉到了立刻吊死。

高纳里尔：　把他的眼珠挖出来。

康华尔：　我自有处置他的办法。爱德蒙，我们不应该让你看见你的谋叛的父亲受到怎样的刑罚，所以请你现在护送我们的姐姐回去，替我向奥本尼公爵致意，叫他赶快准备；我们这儿也要采取同样的行动。我们两地之间，必须随时用飞骑传报消息。再会，亲爱的姐姐；再会，葛罗斯特伯爵。

（奥斯华德上。）

康华尔：　怎么啦？那国王呢？

奥斯华德：　葛罗斯特伯爵已经把他载送出去了；有三十五、六个追寻他的骑士在城门口和他会合，还有几个伯爵手下的人也在一起，一同向多佛进发，据说那边有他们武装的友人在等候他们。

Who, with some other of the lord's dependants,

Are gone with him towards Dover, where they boast

To have well-armed friends.

DUKE OF CORNWALL.　Get horses for your mistress.

GONERIL.　Farewell, sweet lord, and sister.

DUKE OF CORNWALL.　Edmund, farewell.

[*Exeunt Goneril, Edmund, and Oswald.*]

Go seek the traitor Gloster,

Pinion him like a thief, bring him before us.

[*Exeunt other Servants.*]

Though well we may not pass upon his life

Without the form of justice, yet our power

Shall do a court'sy to our wrath, which men

May blame, but not control. Who's there? the traitor?

[*Enter Gloster, brought in by two or three.*]

REGAN.　Ingrateful fox! 'tis he.

DUKE OF CORNWALL.　Bind fast his corky arms.

EARL OF GLOSTER.　What mean, your Graces? Good my friends, consider

You are my guests. Do me no foul play, friends.

DUKE OF CORNWALL.　Bind him, I say.

[*Servants bind him.*]

REGAN.　Hard, hard. O filthy traitor!

EARL OF GLOSTER.　Unmerciful lady as you are, I am none.

康华尔：　替你家夫人备马。

高纳里尔：　再会，殿下，再会，妹妹。

康华尔：　再会，爱德蒙。（高纳里尔、爱德蒙及奥斯华德下。）

再去几个人把那反贼葛罗斯特捉来，像偷儿一样把他绑来见我。（若干仆人下。）虽然在没有经过正式的审判手续以前，我们不能就把他判处死刑，可是为了发泄我们的愤怒，却只好不顾人们的指摘，凭着我们的权力独断独行了。那边是什么人？是那反贼吗？

（众仆押葛罗斯特重上。）

里根：　没有良心的狐狸！正是他。

康华尔：　把他枯瘪的手臂牢牢绑起来。

葛罗斯特：　两位殿下，这是什么意思？我的好朋友们，你们是我的客人；不要用这种无礼的手段对待我。

康华尔：　捆住他。（众仆绑葛罗斯特。）

里根：　绑紧些，绑紧些。啊，可恶的反贼！

葛罗斯特：　你是一个没有心肝的女人，我却不是反贼。

DUKE OF CORNWALL.　To this chair bind him. Villain, thou shalt
　　find –

[*Regan plucks his beard.*]

EARL OF GLOSTER.　By the kind gods, 'tis most ignobly done
　　To pluck me by the beard.

REGAN.　So white, and such a traitor!

EARL OF GLOSTER.　Naughty lady,
　　These hairs which thou dost ravish from my chin
　　Will quicken, and accuse thee. I am your host.
　　With robber's hands my hospitable favours
　　You should not ruffle thus. What will you do?

DUKE OF CORNWALL.　Come, sir, what letters had you late from
　　France?

REGAN.　Be simple-answered, for we know the truth.

DUKE OF CORNWALL.　And what confederacy have you with the
　　traitors
　　Late footed in the kingdom?

REGAN.　To whose hands have you sent the lunatic King?
　　Speak.

EARL OF GLOSTER.　I have a letter guessingly set down,
　　Which came from one that's of a neutral heart,
　　And not from one opposed.

DUKE OF CORNWALL.　Cunning.

REGAN.　And false.

DUKE OF CORNWALL.　Where hast thou sent the King?

康华尔：　把他绑在这张椅子上。奸贼，我要让你知道——

（里根扯葛罗斯特须。）

葛罗斯特：　天神在上，这还成什么话，你扯起我的胡子来啦！

里根：　胡子这么白，想不到却是一个反贼！

葛罗斯特：　恶妇，你从我的腮上扯下这些胡子来，它们将要像活人一样控诉你的罪恶。我是这里的主人，你不该用你强盗的手，这样报答我的好客的殷勤。你究竟要怎么样？

康华尔：　说，你最近从法国得到什么书信？

里根：　老实说出来，我们已经什么都知道了。

康华尔：　你跟那些最近踏到我们国境来的叛徒们有些什么来往？

里根：　你把那发疯的老王送到什么人手里去了？说。

葛罗斯特：　我只收到过一封信，里面都不过是些猜测之谈，寄信的是一个没有偏见的人，并不是一个敌人。

康华尔：　好狡猾的推托！

里根：　一派鬼话！

康华尔：　你把国王送到什么地方去了？

EARL OF GLOSTER.   To Dover.

REGAN.   Wherefore to Dover? Wast thou not charged at peril

DUKE OF CORNWALL.   Wherefore to Dover? Let him first answer
    that.

EARL OF GLOSTER.   I am tied to th' stake, and I must stand the
    course.

REGAN.   Wherefore to Dover, sir?

EARL OF GLOSTER.   Because I would not see thy cruel nails

    Pluck out his poor old eyes; nor thy fierce sister

    In his anointed flesh stick boarish fangs.

    The sea, with such a storm as his bare head

    In hell-black night endured, would have buoyed up

    And quenched the steeled fires.

    Yet, poor old heart, he holp the heavens to rain.

    If wolves had at thy gate howled that stern time,

    Thou shouldst have said, Good Porter, Turn The Key.

    All cruels else subscribed. But I shall see

    The winged vengeance overtake such children.

DUKE OF CORNWALL.   See't shalt thou never.

    Fellows, hold the chair.

    Upon these eyes of thine I'll set my foot.

EARL OF GLOSTER.   He that will think to live till he be old,

    Give me some help! – O cruel! O ye gods!

REGAN.   One side will mock another. Th' other too!

DUKE OF CORNWALL.   If you see vengeance –

1. SERV.   Hold your hand, my lord!

葛罗斯特：　送到多佛。

里根：　为什么送到多佛？我们不是早就警告你——

康华尔：　为什么送到多佛？让他回答这个问题。

葛罗斯特：　罢了，我现在身陷虎穴，只好拼着这条老命了。

里根：　为什么送到多佛？

葛罗斯特：　因为我不愿意看见你的凶恶的指爪挖出他的可怜的老眼；因为我不愿意看见你的残暴的姐姐用她野猪般的利齿咬进他的神圣的肉体。他的赤裸的头顶在地狱一般黑暗的夜里冲风冒雨；受到那样狂风暴雨的震荡的海水，也要把它的怒潮喷向天空，熄灭了星星的火焰；但是他，可怜的老翁，却还要把他的热泪帮助天空浇洒。要是在那样怕人的晚上，豺狼在你的门前悲鸣，你也要说，"善良的看门人，开了门放它进来吧，"而不计较它一切的罪恶。可是我总有一天见到上天的报应降临在这种儿女的身上。

康华尔：　你再也不会见到那样一天。来，按住这椅子。我要把你这一双眼睛放在我的脚底下践踏。

葛罗斯特：　谁要是希望他自己平安活到老年的，帮帮我吧！啊，好惨！天啊！

里根：　还有那一颗眼珠也去掉了吧，免得它嘲笑没有眼珠的一面。

康华尔：　要是你看见什么报应——

仆甲：　住手，殿下；我从小为您效劳，但是只有我现在叫您住手

I have served you ever since I was a child;

But better service have I never done you

Than now to bid you hold.

REGAN.　　How now, you dog?

1. SERV.　　If you did wear a beard upon your chin,

I'ld shake it on this quarrel. What do you mean?

DUKE OF CORNWALL.　　My villain!

[*Draws.*]

1. SERV.　　Nay, then, come on, and take the chance of anger.

[*Draws. They fight. Cornwall is wounded.*]

REGAN.　　Give me thy sword. A peasant stand up thus?

[*She takes a sword and runs at him behind.*]

1. SERV.　　O, I am slain! My lord, you have one eye left

To see some mischief on him. O!

[*He dies.*]

DUKE OF CORNWALL.　　Lest it see more, prevent it.

Out, vile jelly! Where is thy lustre now?

EARL OF GLOSTER.　　All dark and comfortless! Where's my son

Edmund?

Edmund, enkindle all the sparks of nature

To quit this horrid act.

REGAN.　　Out, treacherous villain!

Thou call'st on him that hates thee. It was he

That made the overture of thy treasons to us;

这件事才算是最好的效劳。

里根：　怎么，你这狗东西！

仆甲：　要是你的腮上长起了胡子，我现在也要把它扯下来。

康华尔：　混账奴才，你反了吗？（拔剑。）

仆甲：　好，那么来，我们拼一个你死我活。（拔剑。二人决斗。
康华尔受伤。）

里根：　把你的剑给我。一个奴才也会撒野到这等地步！（取剑自
后刺仆甲。）

仆甲：　啊！我死了。大人，您还剩着一只眼睛，看见他受到一点
小小的报应。啊！（死。）

康华尔：　哼，看他再瞧得见一些什么报应！出来，可恶的浆块！
现在你还会发光吗？（葛罗斯特另一眼被挖出。）

葛罗斯特：　一切都是黑暗和痛苦。我的儿子爱德蒙呢？爱德蒙，
燃起你天性中的怒火，替我报复这一场暗无天日的暴行吧！

里根：　哼，万恶的奸贼！你在呼唤一个憎恨你的人；你对我们反
叛的阴谋，就是他出首告发的，他是一个深明大义的人，绝不
会对你发一点怜悯。

Who is too good to pity thee.

EARL OF GLOSTER.   O my follies!

Then Edgar was abused.

Kind gods, forgive me that, and prosper him!

REGAN.   Go thrust him out at gates, and let him smell

His way to Dover.

[*Exit one with Gloster.*]

How is't, my lord? How look you?

DUKE OF CORNWALL.   I have received a hurt. Follow me, lady.

Turn out that eyeless villain. Throw this slave

Upon the dunghill. Regan, I bleed apace.

Untimely comes this hurt. Give me your arm.

[*Exit Cornwall, led by Regan.*]

2. SERV.   I'll never care what wickedness I do,

If this man come to good.

3. SERV.   If she live long,

And in the end meet the old course of death,

Women will all turn monsters.

2. SERV.   Let's follow the old Earl, and get the bedlam

To lead him where he would. His roguish madness

Allows itself to anything.

3. SERV.   Go thou. I'll fetch some flax and whites of eggs

To apply to his bleeding face. Now heaven help him!

[*Exeunt.*]

葛罗斯特：　啊，我是个蠢材！那么爱德伽是冤枉的了。仁慈的神明啊，赦免我的错误，保佑他有福吧！

里根：　把他推出门外，让他一路摸索到多佛去。（一仆牵葛罗斯特下。）怎么，殿下？您的脸色怎么变啦？

康华尔：　我受了伤啦。跟我来，夫人。把那瞎眼的奸贼撵出去；把这奴才丢在粪堆里。里根，我的血尽在流着；这真是无妄之灾。用你的胳臂搀着我。（里根扶康华尔同下。）

仆乙：　要是这家伙会有好收场，我什么坏事都可以去做了。

仆丙：　要是她会寿终正寝，所有的女人都要变成恶鬼了。

仆乙：　让我们跟在那老伯爵的后面，叫那疯丐把他领到他所要去的地方；反正那个游荡的疯子什么地方都去。

仆丙：　你先去吧；我还要去拿些麻布和蛋白来，替他贴在他的流血的脸上。但愿上天保佑他！（各下。）

ACT IV   SCENE I

The heath.

[*Enter Edgar.*]

EDGAR.   Yet better thus, and known to be contemned,

    Than still contemned and flattered. To be worst,

    The lowest and most dejected thing of fortune,

    Stands still in esperance, lives not in fear.

    The lamentable change is from the best;

    The worst returns to laughter. Welcome then,

    Thou unsubstantial air that I embrace!

    The wretch that thou hast blown unto the worst

    Owes nothing to thy blasts. But who comes here?

    [*Enter Gloster, led by an Old Man.*]

    My father, poorly led? World, world, O world!

    But that thy strange mutations make us hate thee,

    Life would not yield to age.

OLD MAN.   O my good lord, I have been your tenant, and your

    father's tenant,

    These fourscore years.

EARL OF GLOSTER.   Away, get thee away! Good friend, be gone.

    Thy comforts can do me no good at all;

第四幕　第一场

荒野。
（爱德伽上。）

爱德伽：　　与其被人在表面上恭维而背地里鄙弃，那么还是像这样
自己知道为举世所不容的好。一个最困苦、最微贱、最为命运
所屈辱的人，可以永远抱着希冀而无所恐惧；从最高的地位上
跌下来，那变化是可悲的，对于穷困的人，命运的转机却能使
他欢笑！那么欢迎你——跟我拥抱的空虚的气流；被你刮得狼
狈不堪的可怜虫并不少欠你丝毫情分。可是谁来啦？（一老人率
葛罗斯特上。）我的父亲，让一个穷苦的老头儿领着他吗？啊，
世界，世界，世界！倘不是你的变幻无常，使我们对你心存怨
恨，哪一个人是甘愿老去的？

老人：　　啊，我的好老爷！我在老太爷手里就做您府上的佃户，一
直做到您老爷手里，已经有八十年了。

葛罗斯特：　　去吧，好朋友，你快去吧；你的安慰对我一点没有用
处，他们也许反会害你的。

Thee they may hurt.

OLD MAN.   You cannot see your way.

EARL OF GLOSTER.   I have no way, and therefore want no eyes;

I stumbled when I saw. Full oft 'tis seen

Our means secure us, and our mere defects

Prove our commodities. Ah dear son Edgar,

The food of thy abused father's wrath!

Might I but live to see thee in my touch,

I'ld say I had eyes again!

OLD MAN.   How now? Who's there?

EDGAR.   [*Aside.*] O gods! Who is't can say

I am at the worst? I am worse than e'er I was.

OLD MAN.   'Tis poor mad Tom.

EDGAR.   [*Aside.*] And worse I may be yet. The worst is not

So long as we can say This is the worst.

OLD MAN.   Fellow, where goest?

EARL OF GLOSTER.   Is it a beggar-man?

OLD MAN.   Madman and beggar too.

EARL OF GLOSTER.   He has some reason, else he could not beg.

I' th' last night's storm I such a fellow saw,

Which made me think a man a worm. My son

Came then into my mind, and yet my mind

Was then scarce friends with him. I have heard more since.

As flies to wanton boys are we to th' gods.

They kill us for their sport.

EDGAR.   [*Aside.*] How should this be?

老人：　您眼睛看不见，怎么走路呢？

葛罗斯特：　我没有路，所以不需要眼睛；当我能够看见的时候，我也会失足颠扑。我们往往因为有所自恃而失之于大意，反不如缺陷却能对我们有益。啊！爱德伽好儿子，你的父亲受人之愚，错恨了你，要是我能在未死以前，摸到你的身体，我就要说，我又有了眼睛啦。

老人：　啊！那边是什么人？

爱德伽：　（旁白）神啊！谁能够说"我现在是最不幸"？我现在比从前才更不幸得多啦。

老人：　那是可怜的发疯的汤姆。

爱德伽：　（旁白）也许我还要碰到更不幸的命运；当我们能够说"这是最不幸的事"的时候，那还不是最不幸的。

老人：　汉子，你到哪儿去？

葛罗斯特：　是一个叫花子吗？

老人：　是个疯叫花子。

葛罗斯特：　他的理智还没有完全丧失，否则他不会向人乞讨。在昨晚的暴风雨里，我也看见这样一个家伙，他使我想起一个人不过等于一条虫；那时候我的儿子的影像就闪进了我的心里，可是当时我正在恨他，不愿想起他；后来我才听到一些其他的话。天神掌握着我们的命运，正像顽童捉到飞虫一样，为了戏弄的缘故而把我们杀害。

爱德伽：　（旁白）怎么会有这样的事？在一个伤心人的面前装傻，

Bad is the trade that must play fool to sorrow,

Ang'ring itself and others. – Bless thee, master!

EARL OF GLOSTER.   Is that the naked fellow?

OLD MAN.   Ay, my lord.

EARL OF GLOSTER.   Then prithee get thee gone. If for my sake

Thou wilt o'ertake us hence a mile or twain

I' th' way toward Dover, do it for ancient love;

And bring some covering for this naked soul,

Which I'll entreat to lead me.

OLD MAN.   Alack, sir, he is mad!

EARL OF GLOSTER.   'Tis the time's plague when madmen lead the

blind.

Do as I bid thee, or rather do thy pleasure.

Above the rest, be gone.

OLD MAN.   I'll bring him the best 'parel that I have,

Come on't what will.

[*Exit.*]

EARL OF GLOSTER.   Sirrah naked fellow –

EDGAR.   Poor Tom's acold. [*Aside.*] I cannot daub it further.

EARL OF GLOSTER.   Come hither, fellow.

EDGAR.   [*Aside.*] And yet I must. – Bless thy sweet eyes, they bleed.

EARL OF GLOSTER.   Know'st thou the way to Dover?

EDGAR.   Both stile and gate, horseway and footpath. Poor Tom hath

been scared out of his good wits. Bless thee, good man's son, from

the foul fiend! Five fiends have been in poor Tom at once: of lust,

对自己、对别人，都是一件不愉快的行为。（向葛罗斯特）祝
福你，先生！

葛罗斯特：　　他就是那个不穿衣服的家伙吗？

老人：　　正是，老爷。

葛罗斯特：　　那么你去吧。我要请他领我到多佛去，要是你看在我
的份上，愿意回去拿一点衣服来替他遮盖遮盖身体，那就再好
没有了；我们不会走远，从这儿到多佛的路上一二里之内，你
一定可以追上我们。

老人：　　唉，老爷！他是个疯子哩。

葛罗斯特：　　疯子带着瞎子走路，本来是这时代的一般病态。照我
的话，或者就照你自己的意思做吧；第一件事情是请你快去。

老人：　　我要把我的最好的衣服拿来给他，不管它会引起怎样的后
果。（下。）

葛罗斯特：　　喂，不穿衣服的家伙——

爱德伽：　　可怜的汤姆冷着呢。（旁白）我不能再假装下去了。

葛罗斯特：　　过来，汉子。

爱德伽：　　（旁白）可是我不能不假装下去。——祝福您的可爱的
眼睛，它们在流血哩。

葛罗斯特：　　你认识到多佛去的路吗？

爱德伽：　　一处处关口城门、一条条马路人行道，我全认识。可怜
的汤姆被他们吓迷了心窍；祝福你，好人的儿子，愿恶魔不来

lust, as Obidicut; Hobbididence, prince of dumbness; Mahu, of stealing; Modo, of murder; Flibbertigibbet, of mopping and mowing, who since possesses chambermaids and waiting women. So, bless thee, master!

EARL OF GLOSTER.   Here, take this Purse, thou whom the heavens' plagues

Have humbled to all strokes. That I am wretched

Makes thee the happier. Heavens, deal so still!

Let the superfluous and lust-dieted man,

That slaves your ordinance, that will not see

Because he does not feel, feel your pow'r quickly;

So distribution should undo excess,

And each man have enough. Dost thou know Dover?

EDGAR.   Ay, master.

EARL OF GLOSTER.   There is a cliff, whose high and bending head

Looks fearfully in the confined deep.

Bring me but to the very brim of it,

And I'll repair the misery thou dost bear

With something rich about me. From that place

I shall no leading need.

EDGAR.   Give me thy arm.

Poor Tom shall lead thee.

[*Exeunt.*]

缠绕你！五个魔鬼一齐作弄着可怜的汤姆：一个是色魔奥别狄克特；一个是哑鬼霍别狄丹斯；一个是偷东西的玛呼；一个是杀人的摩陀；一个是扮鬼脸的弗力勃铁捷贝特，他后来常常附在丫头、使女的身上。好，祝福您，先生！

葛罗斯特：　来，你这受尽上天凌虐的人，把这钱囊拿去；我的不幸却是你的运气。天道啊，愿你常常如此！让那穷奢极欲、把你的法律当做满足他自己享受的工具、因为知觉麻木而沉迷不悟的人，赶快感到你的威力吧；从享用过度的人手里夺下一点来分给穷人，让每一个人都得到他所应得的一份吧。你认识多佛吗？

爱德伽：　认识，先生。

葛罗斯特：　那边有一座悬崖，它的峭拔的绝顶俯瞰着幽深的海水；你只要领我到那悬崖的边上，我就给你一些我随身携带的贵重的东西，你拿了去可以过些舒服的日子；我也不用再烦你带路了。

爱德伽：　把您的胳臂给我；让可怜的汤姆领着你走。（同下。）

ACT IV   SCENE II

Before the Duke of Albany's Palace.

[Enter Goneril and Edmund the Bastard.]

GONERIL.   Welcome, my lord. I marvel our mild husband

　　Not met us on the way.

　　[Enter Oswald.]

　　Now, where's your master?

OSWALD.   Madam, within, but never man so changed.

　　I told him of the army that was landed:

　　He smiled at it. I told him you were coming:

　　His answer was, The worse. of Gloster's treachery

　　And of the loyal service of his son

　　When I informed him, then he called me sot

　　And told me I had turned the wrong side out.

　　What most he should dislike seems pleasant to him;

　　What like, offensive.

GONERIL.   *[To Edmund.]* Then shall you go no further.

　　It is the cowish terror of his spirit,

　　That dares not undertake. He'll not feel wrongs

　　Which tie him to an answer. Our wishes on the way

　　May prove effects. Back, Edmund, to my brother.

第四幕　第二场

奥本尼公爵府前。

（高纳里尔及爱德蒙上。）

高纳里尔：　欢迎，伯爵；我不知道我那位温和的丈夫为什么不来
　　　　迎接我们。（奥斯华德上。）主人呢？

奥斯华德：　夫人，他在里边；可是已经大大变了一个人啦。我告
　　　　诉他法国军队登陆的消息，他听了只是微笑；我告诉他说您来
　　　　了，他的回答却是，"还是不来的好"；我告诉他葛罗斯特怎
　　　　样谋反、他的儿子怎样尽忠的时候，他骂我蠢东西，说我颠倒
　　　　是非。凡是他所应该痛恨的事情，他听了都觉得很得意；他所
　　　　应该欣慰的事情，反而使他恼怒。

高纳里尔：　（向爱德蒙）那么你止步吧。这是他懦怯畏缩的天性，
　　　　使他不敢担当大事；他宁愿忍受侮辱，不肯挺身而起。我们在
　　　　路上谈起的那个愿望，也许可以实现。爱德蒙，你且回到我的
　　　　妹夫那儿去；催促他赶紧调齐人马，交给你统率；我这儿只好
　　　　由我自己出马，把家务托付我的丈夫照管了。这个可靠的仆人

Hasten his musters and conduct his powers.

I must change arms at home and give the distaff

Into my husband's hands. This trusty servant

Shall pass between us. Ere long you are like to hear

If you dare venture in your own behalf

A mistress's command. Wear this. Spare speech.

[*Gives a favour.*].

Decline your head. This kiss, if it durst speak,

Would stretch thy spirits up into the air.

Conceive, and fare thee well.

EDMUND.   Yours in the ranks of death!

GONERIL.   My most dear Gloster! [*Exit Edmund.*]

O, the difference of man and man! To thee

A woman's services are due; My fool

Usurps my body.

OSWALD.   Madam, here comes my lord.

[*Exit.*]

[*Enter Albany.*]

GONERIL.   I have been worth the whistle.

DUKE OF ALBANY.   O Goneril,

You are not worth the dust which the rude wind

Blows in your face! I fear your disposition.

That nature which contemns it origin

可以替我们传达消息；要是你有胆量为了你自己的好处而行事，那么不久大概就会听到你的女主人的命令。把这东西拿去带在身边；不要多说什么；（以饰物赠爱德蒙。）低下你的头来：这一个吻要是能够替我说话，它会叫你的灵魂儿飞上天空的。你要明白我的心；再会吧。

爱德蒙：　我愿意为您赴汤蹈火。

高纳里尔：　我的最亲爱的葛罗斯特！（爱德蒙下。）唉！都是男人，却有这样的不同！哪一个女人不愿意为你贡献她的一切，我却让一个傻瓜侵占了我的眠床。

奥斯华德：　夫人，殿下来了。（下。）

（奥本尼上。）

高纳里尔：　你太瞧不起人啦。

奥本尼：　啊，高纳里尔！你的价值还比不上那狂风吹在你脸上的尘土。我替你这种脾气担着心事；一个人要是看轻了自己的根本，难免做出一些越限逾分的事来；枝叶脱离了树干，跟着也要萎谢，到后来只好让人当做枯柴而付之一炬。

Cannot be bordered certain in itself.

She that herself will sliver and disbranch

From her material sap, perforce must wither

And come to deadly use.

GONERIL.　No more! The text is foolish.

DUKE OF ALBANY.　Wisdom and goodness to the vile seem vile;

Filths savour but themselves. What have you done?

Tigers, not daughters, what have you performed?

A father, and a gracious aged man,

Whose reverence even the head-lugged bear would lick,

Most barbarous, most degenerate, have you madded.

Could my good brother suffer you to do it?

A man, a prince, by him so benefited!

If that the heavens do not their visible spirits

Send quickly down to tame these vile offences,

It will come,

Humanity must perforce prey on itself,

Like monsters of the deep.

GONERIL.　Milk-livered man!

That bear'st a cheek for blows, a head for wrongs;

Who hast not in thy brows an eye discerning

Thine honour from thy suffering; that not know'st

Fools do those villains pity who are punished

Ere they have done their mischief. Where's thy drum?

France spreads his banners in our noiseless land,

高纳里尔：　　得啦得啦；全是些傻话。

奥本尼：　　智慧和仁义在恶人眼中看来都是恶的；下流的人只喜欢
　　下流的事。你们干下了些什么事情？你们是猛虎，不是女儿，
　　你们干了些什么事啦？这样一位父亲，这样一位仁慈的老人家，
　　一头野熊见了他也会俯首帖耳，你们这些蛮横下贱的女儿，却
　　把他激成了疯狂！难道我那位贤婿兄竟会让你们这样胡闹吗？
　　他也是个堂堂汉子，一邦的君主，又受过他这样的深恩厚德！
　　要是上天不立刻降下一些明显的灾祸来，惩罚这种万恶的行为，
　　那么人类快要像深海的怪物一样自相吞食了。

高纳里尔：　　不中用的懦夫！你让人家打肿你的脸，把侮辱加在你
　　的头上，还以为是一件体面的事，因为你的额头上还没长着眼
　　睛；正像那些不明是非的傻瓜，人家存心害你，幸亏发觉得早，
　　他们在未下毒手以前就受到惩罚，你却还要可怜他们。你的鼓
　　呢？法国的旌旗已经展开在我们安静的国境上了，你的敌人顶
　　着羽毛飘扬的战盔，已经开始威胁你的生命。你这迂腐的傻子
　　却坐着一动不动，只会说，"唉！他为什么要这样呢？"

With plumed helm thy state begins to threat,

Whiles thou, a moral fool, sit'st still, and cries

Alack, why does he so?

DUKE OF ALBANY.　See thyself, devil!

Proper deformity seems not in the fiend

So horrid as in woman.

GONERIL.　O vain fool!

DUKE OF ALBANY.　Thou changèd and self-covered thing, for shame!

Be-monster not thy feature! Were't my fitness

To let these hands obey my blood,

They are apt enough to dislocate and tear

Thy flesh and bones. Howe'er thou art a fiend,

A woman's shape doth shield thee.

GONERIL.　Marry, your manhood mew!

[*Enter a Gentleman.*]

DUKE OF ALBANY.　What news?

GENTLEMAN.　O, my good lord, the Duke of Cornwall 's dead,

Slain by his servant, going to put out

The other eye of Gloster.

DUKE OF ALBANY.　Gloster's eyes?

GENTLEMAN.　A servant that he bred, thrilled with remorse,

Opposed against the act, bending his sword

奥本尼：　　瞧瞧你自己吧，魔鬼！恶魔的丑恶的嘴脸，还不及一个恶魔般的女人那样丑恶万分。

高纳里尔：　　哎哟，你这没有头脑的蠢货！

奥本尼：　　你这变化做女人的形状、掩蔽你的蛇蝎般的真相的魔鬼，不要露出你的狰狞的面目来吧！要是我可以允许这双手服从我的怒气，它们一定会把你的肉一块块撕下来，把你的骨头一根根折断；可是你虽然是一个魔鬼，你的形状却还是一个女人，我不能伤害你。

高纳里尔：　　哼，这就是你的男子汉的气概。——呸！

（一使者上。）

奥本尼：　　有什么消息？

使者：　　啊！殿下，康华尔公爵死了；他正要挖去葛罗斯特第二只眼睛的时候，他的一个仆人把他杀死了。

奥本尼：　　葛罗斯特的眼睛！

使者：　　他所畜养的一个仆人因为激于义愤，反对他这一种行动，就拔出剑来向他的主人行刺；他的主人大怒，和他奋力猛斗，

To his great master; who, thereat enraged,

Flew on him, and amongst them felled him dead;

But not without that harmful stroke which since

Hath plucked him after.

DUKE OF ALBANY.   This shows you are above,

You justicers, that these our nether crimes

So speedily can venge! But O poor Gloster!

Lose he his other eye?

GENTLEMAN.   Both, both, my lord.

This letter, madam, craves a speedy answer.

'Tis from your sister.

GONERIL.   [*Aside.*] One way I like this well;

But being widow, and my Gloster with her,

May all the building in my fancy pluck

Upon my hateful life. Another way

The news is not so tart. – I'll read, and answer.

[*Exit.*]

DUKE OF ALBANY.   Where was his son when they did take his eyes?

GENTLEMAN.   Come with my lady hither.

DUKE OF ALBANY.   He is not here.

GENTLEMAN.   No, my good lord; I met him back again.

DUKE OF ALBANY.   Knows he the wickedness?

GENTLEMAN.   Ay, my good lord. 'Twas he informed against him,

结果把那仆人砍死了，可是自己也受了重伤，终于不治身亡。

奥本尼：　啊，天道究竟还是有的，人世的罪恶这样快就受到了诛谴！但是啊，可怜的葛罗斯特！他失去了他的第二只眼睛吗？

使者：　殿下，他两只眼睛全都给挖去了。夫人，这一封信是您的妹妹写来的，请您立刻给她一个回音。

高纳里尔：　（旁白）从一方面说来，这是一个好消息；可是她做了寡妇，我的葛罗斯特又跟她在一起，也许我的一切美满的愿望，都要从我这可憎的生命中消灭了；不然的话，这消息还不算顶坏。（向使者）我读过以后再写回信吧。（下。）

奥本尼：　他们挖去他的眼睛的时候，他的儿子在什么地方？
使者：　他是跟夫人一起到这儿来的。
奥本尼：　他不在这儿。
使者：　是的，殿下，我在路上碰见他回去了。
奥本尼：　他知道这种罪恶的事情吗？
使者：　是，殿下；就是他出首告发他的，他故意离开那座房屋，

And quit the house on purpose, that their punishment

Might have the freer course.

DUKE OF ALBANY.　Gloster, I live

To thank thee for the love thou showedst the King,

And to revenge thine eyes. Come hither, friend.

Tell me what more thou know'st.

[*Exeunt.*]

为的是让他们行事方便一些。

奥本尼：　　葛罗斯特，我永远感激你对王上所表示的好意，一定替你报复你的挖目之仇。过来，朋友，详细告诉我一些你所知道的其他的消息。（同下。）

ACT IV   SCENE III

The French camp near Dover.
[*Enter Kent and a Gentleman.*]

EARL OF KENT.   Why the King of France is so suddenly gone back
    know you the reason?

GENTLEMAN.   Something he left imperfect in the state, which since
    his coming forth is thought of, which imports to the kingdom so
    much fear and danger that his personal return was most required
    and necessary.

EARL OF KENT.   Who hath he left behind him general?

GENTLEMAN.   The Marshal of France, Monsieur La Far.

EARL OF KENT.   Did your letters pierce the Queen to any
    demonstration of grief?

GENTLEMAN.   Ay, sir. She took them, read them in my presence,
    And now and then an ample tear trilled down
    Her delicate cheek. It seemed she was a queen
    Over her passion, who, most rebel-like,
    Sought to be king o'er her.

EARL OF KENT.   O, then it moved her?

GENTLEMAN.   Not to a rage. Patience and sorrow strove
    Who should express her goodliest. You have seen

第四幕　第三场

多佛附近法军营地。

（肯特及一侍臣上。）

肯特：　为什么法兰西王突然回去，您知道他的理由吗？

侍臣：　他在国内还有一点未了的要事，直到离国以后，方才想起；
　　　　因为那件事情有关国家的安全，所以他不能不亲自回去料理。

肯特：　他去了以后，委托什么人代他主持军务？

侍臣：　拉·发元帅。

肯特：　王后看了您的信，有没有什么悲哀的表示？

侍臣：　是的，先生；她拿了信，当着我的面前读下去，一颗颗饱
　　　　满的泪珠淌下她的娇嫩的颊上；可是她仍然保持着一个王后的
　　　　尊严，虽然她的情感像叛徒一样想要把她压服，她还是竭力把
　　　　它克制下去。

肯特：　啊！那么她是受到感动的了。

侍臣：　她并不痛哭流涕；"忍耐"和"悲哀"互相竞争着谁能把
　　　　她表现得更美。您曾经看见过阳光和雨点同时出现；她的微笑

Sunshine and rain at once: her smiles and tears

Were like, a better way. Those happy smilets

That played on her ripe lip seemed not to know

What guests were in her eyes, which parted thence

As pearls from diamonds dropped. In brief,

Sorrow would be a rarity most beloved,

If all could so become it.

EARL OF KENT.　Made she no verbal question?

GENTLEMAN.　Faith, once or twice she heaved the name of father

Pantingly forth, as if it pressed her heart;

Cried Sisters, sisters! Shame of ladies! Sisters!

Kent! father! sisters! What, i' th' storm? i' th' night?

Let pity not be believed! There she shook

The holy water from her heavenly eyes,

And clamour moistened. Then away she started

To deal with grief alone.

EARL OF KENT.　It is the stars,

The stars above us, govern our conditions;

Else one self mate and mate could not beget

Such different issues. You spoke not with her since?

GENTLEMAN.　No.

EARL OF KENT.　Was this before the King returned?

GENTLEMAN.　No, since.

EARL OF KENT.　Well, sir, the poor distressed Lear's i' th' town;

Who sometime, in his better tune, remembers

What we are come about, and by no means

和眼泪也正是这样，只是更要动人得多；那些荡漾在她的红润
的嘴唇上的小小的微笑，似乎不知道她的眼睛里有些什么客人，
他们从她钻石一样晶莹的眼球里滚出来，正像一颗颗浑圆的珍
珠。简单一句话，要是所有的悲哀都是这样美，那么悲哀将要
成为最受世人喜爱的珍奇了。

肯特：　她没有说过什么话吗？

侍臣：　一两次她的嘴里迸出了"父亲"两个字，好像它们重压着
　　　　她的心一般；她哀呼着，"姐姐！姐姐！女人的耻辱！姐姐！
　　　　肯特！父亲！姐姐！什么，在风雨里吗？在黑夜里吗？不要相
　　　　信世上还有怜悯吧！"于是她挥去了她的天仙一般的眼睛里的
　　　　神圣的水珠，让眼泪淹没了她的沉痛的悲号，移步他往，和哀
　　　　愁独自做伴去了。

肯特：　那是天上的星辰，天上的星辰主宰着我们的命运；否则同
　　　　一个父母怎么会生出这样不同的儿女来。您后来没有跟她说过
　　　　话吗？

侍臣：　没有。

肯特：　这是在法兰西王回国以前的事吗？

侍臣：　不，这是他去后的事。

肯特：　好，告诉您吧，可怜的受难的李尔已经到了此地，他在比
　　　　较清醒的时候，知道我们来干什么事，一定不肯见他的女儿。

Will yield to see his daughter.

GENTLEMAN.　Why, good sir?

EARL OF KENT.　A sovereign shame so elbows him; his own unkindness,

That stripped her from his benediction, turned her

To foreign casualties, gave her dear rights

To his dog-hearted daughters – these things sting

His mind so venomously that burning shame

Detains him from Cordelia.

GENTLEMAN.　Alack, poor gentleman!

EARL OF KENT.　Of Albany's and Cornwall's powers you heard not?

GENTLEMAN.　'Tis so; they are afoot.

EARL OF KENT.　Well, sir, I'll bring you to our master Lear

And leave you to attend him. Some dear cause

Will in concealment wrap me up awhile.

When I am known aright, you shall not grieve

Lending me this acquaintance. I pray you go

Along with me.

[*Exeunt.*]

侍臣：　为什么呢，好先生？

肯特：　羞耻之心掣住了他；他自己的忍心剥夺了她的应得的慈爱，使她远适异国，听任天命的安排，把她的权利分给那两个犬狼之心的女儿——这种种的回忆像毒刺一样蛰着他的心，使他充满了火烧一样的惭愧，阻止他和考狄利娅相见。

侍臣：　唉！可怜的人！

肯特：　关于奥本尼和康华尔的军队，您听见什么消息没有？

侍臣：　是的，他们已经出动了。

肯特：　好，先生，我要带您去见见我们的王上，请您替我照料照料他。我因为有某种重要的理由，必须暂时隐藏我的真相；当您知道我是什么人以后，您绝不会后悔跟我结识的。请您跟我走吧。（同下。）

ACT IV   SCENE IV

The same. A tent.

[*Enter, with drum and colours, Cordelia, Doctor, and Soldiers.*]

CORDELIA.   Alack, 'tis he! Why, he was met even now

    As mad as the vexed sea, singing aloud,

    Crowned with rank fumiter and furrow weeds,

    With harlocks, hemlock, nettles, cuckoo flowers,

    Darnel, and all the idle weeds that grow

    In our sustaining corn. A century send forth.

    Search every acre in the high-grown field

    And bring him to our eye.

    [*Exit an Officer.*]

    What can man's wisdom

    In the restoring his bereaved sense?

    He that helps him take all my outward worth.

DOCTOR.   There is means, madam.

    Our foster nurse of nature is repose,

    The which he lacks. That to provoke in him

    Are many simples operative, whose power

    Will close the eye of anguish.

CORDELIA.   All blest secrets,

第四幕　第四场

同前。帐幕。

（旗鼓前导，考狄利娅、医生及兵士等上。）

考狄利娅：　唉！正是他。刚才还有人看见他，疯狂得像被飓风激动的怒海，高声歌唱，头上插满了恶臭的地烟草、牛蒡、毒芹、荨麻、杜鹃花和各种蔓生在田亩间的野草。派一百个兵士到繁茂的田野里各处搜寻，把他领来见我。（一军官下。）人们的智慧能不能恢复他的丧失的心神？谁要是能够医治他，我愿意把我的身外的富贵一起送给他。

医生：　娘娘，法子是有的；休息是滋养疲乏的精神的保姆，他现在就是缺少休息；只要给他服一些药草，就可以阖上他的痛苦的眼睛。

考狄利娅：　一切神圣的秘密、一切地下潜伏的灵奇，随着我的眼

All you unpublished virtues of the earth,

Spring with my tears! be aidant and remediate

In the good man's distress! Seek, seek for him!

Lest his ungoverned rage dissolve the life

That wants the means to lead it.

[*Enter Messenger.*]

MESS.   News, madam.

The British powers are marching hitherward.

CORDELIA.   'Tis known before. Our preparation stands

In expectation of them. O dear father,

It is thy business that I go about.

Therefore great France

My mourning and important tears hath pitied.

No blown ambition doth our arms incite,

But love, dear love, and our aged father's right.

Soon may I hear and see him!

[*Exeunt.*]

泪一起奔涌出来吧！帮助解除我的善良的父亲的痛苦！快去找他，快去找他，我只怕他在不可控制的疯狂之中会消灭了他的失去主宰的生命。

（一使者上。）

使者： 报告娘娘，英国军队向这儿开过来了。

考狄利娅： 我们早已知道；一切都预备好了，只等他们到来。亲爱的父亲啊！我这次掀动干戈，完全是为了你的缘故；伟大的法兰西王被我的悲哀和恳求的眼泪所感动。我们出师，并非怀着什么非分的野心，只是一片真情，热烈的真情，要替我们的老父主持正义。但愿我不久就可以听见看见他！（同下。）

ACT IV   SCENE V

Gloster's Castle.

[*Enter Regan and Oswald the Steward.*]

REGAN.   But are my brother's powers set forth?

OSWALD.   Ay, madam.

REGAN.   Himself in person there?

OSWALD.   Madam, with much ado. Your sister is the better soldier.

REGAN.   Lord Edmund spake not with your lord at home?

OSWALD.   No, madam.

REGAN.   What might import my sister's letter to him?

OSWALD.   I know not, lady.

REGAN.   Faith, he is posted hence on serious matter.

    It was great ignorance, Gloster's eyes being out,

    To let him live. Where he arrives he moves

    All hearts against us. Edmund, I think, is gone,

    In pity of his misery, to dispatch

    His nighted life; moreover, to descry

    The strength o' th' enemy.

OSWALD.   I must needs after him, madam, with my letter.

REGAN.   Our troops set forth to-morrow. Stay with us.

    The ways are dangerous.

第四幕　第五场

葛罗斯特城堡中一室。

（里根及奥斯华德上。）

里根：　　可是我的姐夫的军队已经出发了吗？

奥斯华德：　　出发了，夫人。

里根：　　他亲自率领吗？

奥斯华德：　　夫人，好容易才把他催上了马；还是您的姐姐是个更好的军人哩。

里根：　　爱德蒙伯爵到了你们家里，有没有跟你家主人谈过话？

奥斯华德：　　没有，夫人。

里根：　　我的姐姐给他的信里有些什么话？

奥斯华德：　　我不知道，夫人。

里根：　　告诉你吧，他有重要的事情，已经离开此地了。葛罗斯特被挖去了眼睛以后，仍旧放他活命，实在是一个极大的失策；因为他每到一个地方，都会激起众人对我们的反感。我想爱德蒙因为怜悯他的苦难，是要去替他解脱他的暗无天日的生涯的；而且他还负有探察敌人实力的使命。

奥斯华德：　　夫人，我必须追上去把我的信送给他。

里根：　　我们的军队明天就要出发；你暂时耽搁在我们这儿吧，路上很危险呢。

OSWALD. I may not, madam. My lady charged my duty in this business.

REGAN. Why should she write to Edmund? Might not you
Transport her purposes by word? Belike,
Something – I know not what – I'll love thee much –
Let me unseal the letter.

OSWALD. Madam, I had rather –

REGAN. I know your lady does not love her husband;
I am sure of that; and at her late being here
She gave strange eyeliads and most speaking looks
To noble Edmund. I know you are of her bosom.

OSWALD. I, madam?

REGAN. I speak in understanding. Y'are! I know't.
Therefore I do advise you take this note.
My lord is dead; Edmund and I have talked,
And more convenient is he for my hand
Than for your lady's. You may gather more.
If you do find him, pray you give him this;
And when your mistress hears thus much from you,
I pray desire her call her wisdom to her.
So farewell.
If you do chance to hear of that blind traitor,
Preferment falls on him that cuts him off.

OSWALD. Would I could meet him, madam! I should show
What party I do follow.

REGAN. Fare thee well. [*Exeunt.*]

奥斯华德：　我不能，夫人；我家夫人曾经吩咐我不准误事的。

里根：　为什么她要写信给爱德蒙呢？难道你不能替她口头传达她的意思吗？看来恐怕有点儿——我也说不出来。让我拆开这封信来，我会十分喜欢你的。

奥斯华德：　夫人，那我可——

里根：　我知道你家夫人不爱她的丈夫；这一点我是可以确定的。她最近在这儿的时候，常常对高贵的爱德蒙抛掷含情的媚眼。我知道你是她的心腹之人。

奥斯华德：　我，夫人！

里根：　我的话不是随便说说的，我知道你是她的心腹；所以你且听我说，我的丈夫已经死了，爱德蒙跟我曾经谈起过，他向我求爱总比向你家夫人求爱来得方便些。其余的你自己去意会吧。要是你找到了他，请你替我把这个交给他；你把我的话对你家夫人说了以后，再请她仔细想个明白。好，再会。假如你听见人家说起那瞎眼的老贼在什么地方，能够把他除掉，一定可以得到重赏。

奥斯华德：　但愿他能够碰在我的手里，夫人；我一定可以向您表明我是哪一方面的人。

里根：　再会。（各下。）

ACT IV   SCENE VI

The country near Dover.

[*Enter Gloster, and Edgar like a Peasant.*]

EARL OF GLOSTER.   When shall I come to th' top of that same hill?

EDGAR.   You do climb up it now. Look how we labour.

EARL OF GLOSTER.   Me thinks the ground is even.

EDGAR.   Horrible steep. Hark, do you hear the sea?

EARL OF GLOSTER.   No, truly.

EDGAR.   Why, then, your other senses grow imperfect
   By your eyes' anguish.

EARL OF GLOSTER.   So may it be indeed.
   Methinks thy voice is altered, and thou speak'st
   In better phrase and matter than thou didst.

EDGAR.   You are much deceived. In nothing am I changed
   But in my garments.

EARL OF GLOSTER.   Methinks y'are better spoken.

EDGAR.   Come on, sir; here's the place. Stand still. How fearful
   And dizzy 'tis to cast one's eyes so low!
   The crows and choughs that wing the midway air
   Show scarce so gross as beetles. Half way down
   Hangs one that gathers samphire – dreadful trade!

第四幕　第六场

多佛附近的乡间。

（葛罗斯特及爱德伽作农民装束同上。）

葛罗斯特：　什么时候我才能够登上山顶？

爱德伽：　您现在正在一步步上去；瞧这路多么难走。

葛罗斯特：　我觉得这地面是很平的。

爱德伽：　陡峭得可怕呢；听！那不是海水的声音吗？

葛罗斯特：　不，我真的听不见。

爱德伽：　哎哟，那么大概因为您的眼睛痛得厉害，所以别的知觉
也连带模糊起来啦。

葛罗斯特：　那倒也许是真的。我觉得你的声音也变了样啦，你讲
的话不像原来那样粗鲁、那样疯疯癫癫啦。

爱德伽：　您错啦；除了我的衣服以外，我什么都没有变样。

葛罗斯特：　我觉得你的话像样得多啦。

爱德伽：　来，先生；我们已经到了，您站好。把眼睛一直望到这
么低的地方，真是惊心炫目！在半空盘旋的乌鸦，瞧上去还没
有甲虫那么大；山腰中间悬着一个采金花草的人，可怕的工作！
我看他的全身简直抵不上一个人头的大小。在海滩上走路的渔
夫就像小鼠一般，那艘待泊在岸旁的高大的帆船小得像它的划

Methinks he seems no bigger than his head.

The fishermen that walk upon the beach

Appear like mice; and yond tall anchoring bark,

Diminished to her cock; her cock, a buoy

Almost too small for sight. The murmuring surge

That on th' unnumb'red idle pebble chafes

Cannot be heard so high. I'll look no more,

Lest my brain turn, and the deficient sight

Topple down headlong.

EARL OF GLOSTER.　Set me where you stand.

EDGAR.　Give me your hand.

You are now within a foot

Of th' extreme verge. For all beneath the moon

Would I not leap upright.

EARL OF GLOSTER.　Let go my hand.

Here, friend, is another purse; in it a jewel

Well worth a poor man's taking. Fairies and gods

Prosper it with thee! Go thou further off;

Bid me farewell, and let me hear thee going.

EDGAR.　Now fare ye well, good sir.

EARL OF GLOSTER.　With all my heart.

EDGAR.　[*Aside.*] Why I do trifle thus with his despair

Is done to cure it.

EARL OF GLOSTER.　O you mighty gods!

[*He kneels.*]

This world I do renounce, and, in your sights,

艇，它的划艇小得像一个浮标，几乎看不出来。澎湃的波涛在海滨无数的石子上冲击的声音，也不能传到这样高的所在。我不愿再看下去了，恐怕我的头脑要昏眩起来，眼睛一花，就要一个筋斗直跌下去。

葛罗斯特：　带我到你所立的地方。

爱德伽：　把您的手给我；您现在已经离开悬崖的边上只有一英尺了；谁要是把天下所有的一切都给了我，我也不愿意跳下去。

葛罗斯特：　放开我的手。朋友，这儿又是一个钱囊，里面有一颗宝石，一个穷人得到了它，可以终身温饱；愿天神们保佑你因此而得福吧！你再走远一点；向我告别一声，让我听见你走过去。

爱德伽：　再会吧，好先生。

葛罗斯特：　再会。

爱德伽：　（旁白）我这样戏弄他的目的，是要把他从绝望的境界中解救出来。

葛罗斯特：　威严的神明啊！（向前扑地。）我现在脱离这一个世界，当着你们的面，摆脱我的残酷的痛苦了；要是我能够再忍受下去，而不怨尤你们不可反抗的伟大意志，我这可厌的生命

Shake patiently my great affliction off.

If I could bear it longer and not fall

To quarrel with your great opposeless wills,

My snuff and loathed part of nature should

Burn itself out. If Edgar live, O, bless him!

Now, fellow, fare thee well.

EDGAR.   Gone, sir, farewell.

[*Gloster falls forward.*]

[*Aside.*] And yet I know not how conceit may rob

The treasury of life when life itself

Yields to the theft. Had he been where he thought,

By this had thought been past. – Alive or dead?

Ho you, sir! friend! Hear you, sir? Speak! –

Thus might he pass indeed. Yet he revives.

What are you, sir?

EARL OF GLOSTER.   Away, and let me die.

EDGAR.   Hadst thou been aught but gossamer, feathers, air,

So many fathom down precipitating,

Thouedst shivered like an egg; but thou dost breathe;

Hast heavy substance; bleed'st not; speak'st; art sound.

Ten masts at each make not the altitude

Which thou hast perpendicularly fell.

Thy life is a miracle. Speak yet again.

EARL OF GLOSTER.   But have I fallen, or no?

EDGAR.   From the dread summit of this chalky bourn.

Look up a-height. The shrill-gorged lark so far

的余烬不久也会燃尽的。要是爱德伽尚在人世，神啊，请你们
祝福他！现在，朋友，我们再会了！

爱德伽：　　我去了，先生；再会。（旁白）可是我不知道当一个人
　　　　愿意受他自己的幻想的欺骗，相信他已经死去的时候，那一种
　　　　幻想会不会真的偷去了他的生命的至宝；要是他果然在他所想
　　　　象的那一个地方，现在他早已没有思想了。活着还是死了？（向
　　　　葛罗斯特）喂，你这位先生！朋友！你听见吗，先生？说呀！
　　　　也许他真的死了；可是他醒过来啦。你是什么人，先生？

葛罗斯特：　　去，让我死。
爱德伽：　　倘使你不是一根蛛丝、一根羽毛、一阵空气，从这样千
　　　　仞的悬崖上跌落下来，早就像鸡蛋一样跌成粉碎了；可是你还
　　　　在呼吸，你的身体还是好好的，不流一滴血，还会说话，简直
　　　　一点损伤也没有。十根桅杆连接起来，也不及你所跌下来的地
　　　　方那么高；你的生命是一个奇迹。再对我说两句话吧。

葛罗斯特：　　可是我有没有跌下来？
爱德伽：　　你就是从这可怕的悬崖绝顶上面跌下来的。抬起头来看
　　　　一看吧；鸣声嘹亮的云雀飞到了那样高的所在，我们不但看不

Cannot be seen or heard. Do but look up.

EARL OF GLOSTER.   Alack, I have no eyes!

Is wretchedness deprived that benefit

To end itself by death? 'Twas yet some comfort

When misery could beguile the tyrant's rage

And frustrate his proud will.

EDGAR.   Give me your arm.

Up – so. How is't? Feel you your legs? You stand.

EARL OF GLOSTER.   Too well, too well.

EDGAR.   This is above all strangeness.

Upon the crown o' th' cliff what thing was that

Which parted from you?

EARL OF GLOSTER.   A poor unfortunate beggar.

EDGAR.   As I stood here below, methought his eyes

Were two full moons; he had a thousand noses,

Horns whelked and waved like the enridgèd sea.

It was some fiend. Therefore, thou happy father,

Think that the clearest gods, who make them honours

Of men's impossibility, have preserved thee.

EARL OF GLOSTER.   I do remember now. Henceforth I'll bear

Affliction till it do cry out itself

Enough, enough, and die. That thing you speak of,

I took it for a man. Often 'twould say

The fiend, the fiend – he led me to that place.

EDGAR.   Ear free and patient thoughts.

见它的形状，也听不见它的声音；你看。

葛罗斯特：　唉！我没有眼睛哩。难道一个苦命的人，连寻死的权利都要被剥夺去吗？一个苦恼到极点的人假使还有办法对付那暴君的狂怒，挫败他的骄傲的意志，那么他多少还有一点可以自慰。

爱德伽：　把你的胳臂给我；起来，好，怎样？站得稳吗？你站住了。

葛罗斯特：　很稳，很稳。

爱德伽：　这真太不可思议了。刚才在那悬崖的顶上，从你身边走开的是什么东西？

葛罗斯特：　一个可怜的叫花子。

爱德伽：　我站在下面望着他，仿佛看见他的眼睛像两轮满月；他有一千个鼻子，满头都是像波浪一样高低不齐的犄角；一定是个什么恶魔。所以，你幸运的老人家，你应该想这是无所不能的神明在暗中默佑你，否则绝不会有这样的奇事。

葛罗斯特：　我现在记起来了；从此以后，我要耐心忍受痛苦，直等它有一天自己喊了出来，"够啦，够啦，"那时候再撒手死去。你所说起的这一个东西，我还以为是个人；它老是嚷着"恶魔，恶魔"的；就是他把我领到了那个地方。

爱德伽：　不要胡思乱想，安心忍耐。可是谁来啦？

[*Enter Lear, fantastically dressed with wild flowers.*]

EDGAR.　But who comes here?

　　The safer sense will ne'er accommodate

　　His master thus.

KING LEAR.　No, they cannot touch me for coming; I am the King himself.

EDGAR.　O thou side-piercing sight!

KING LEAR.　Nature 's above art in that respect. There's your press money. That fellow handles his bow like a crow-keeper. Draw me a clothier's yard. Look, look, a mouse! Peace, peace; this piece of toasted cheese will do't. There's my gauntlet; I'll prove it on a giant. Bring up the brown bills. O, well flown, bird! i' th' clout, i' th' clout: hewgh! Give the word.

EDGAR.　Sweet marjoram.

KING LEAR.　Pass.

EARL OF GLOSTER.　I know that voice.

KING LEAR.　Ha! Goneril with a white beard? They flattered me like a dog, and told me I had white hairs in my beard ere the black ones were there. To say ay and no to everything I said! Ay and no too was no good divinity. When the rain came to wet me once, and the wind to make me chatter; when the thunder would not peace at my bidding; there I found 'em, there I smelt 'em out. Go to, they are not men o' their words! They told me I was everything. 'Tis a lie – I am not ague-proof.

EARL OF GLOSTER.　The trick of that voice I do well remember. Is't not the King?

（李尔以鲜花杂乱饰身上。）

爱德伽：　　不是疯狂的人，绝不会把他自己打扮成这一个样子。

李尔：　　不，他们不能判我私造货币的罪名；我是国王哩。

爱德伽：　　啊，伤心的景象！

李尔：　　在那一点上，天然是胜过人工的。这是征募你们当兵的饷银。那家伙弯弓的姿势，活像一个稻草人；给我射一支一码长的箭试试看。瞧，瞧！一只小老鼠！别闹，别闹！这一块烘乳酪可以捉住它。这是我的铁手套；尽管他是一个巨人，我也要跟他一决胜负。带那些戟手上来。啊！飞得好，鸟儿；刚刚中在靶子心里，啾！口令！

爱德伽：　　茉荞兰。

李尔：　　过去。

葛罗斯特：　　我认识那个声音。

李尔：　　嘿！高纳里尔，长着一把白胡须！她们像狗一样向我献媚。说我在没有出黑须以前，就已经有了白须。我说一声"是"，她们就应一声"是"；我说一声"不"，她们就应一声"不"！当雨点淋湿了我，风吹得我牙齿打颤，当雷声不肯听我的话平静下来的时候，我才发现了她们，嗅出了她们。算了，她们不是心口如一的人；她们把我恭维得天花乱坠；全然是个谎，一发起烧来我就没有办法。

葛罗斯特：　　这一种说话的声调我记得很清楚；他不是我们的君王吗？

KING LEAR.   Ay, every inch a king!

> When I do stare, see how the subject quakes.

> I pardon that man's life. What was thy cause? Adultery?

> Thou shalt not die. Die for adultery? No.

> The wren goes to't, and the small gilded fly

> Does lecher in my sight.

> Let copulation thrive; for Gloster's bastard son

> Was kinder to his father than my daughters

> Got 'tween the lawful sheets.

> To't, luxury, pell-mell! for I lack soldiers.

> Behold yond simp'ring dame,

> Whose face between her forks presages snow,

> That minces virtue, and does shake the head

> To hear of pleasure's name.

> The fitchew nor the soiled horse goes to't

> With a more riotous appetite.

> Down from the waist they are Centaurs,

> Though women all above.

> But to the girdle do the gods inherit,

> Beneath is all the fiend's.

> There's hell, there's darkness, there's the sulphurous pit;

> burning, scalding, stench, consumption.

> Fie, fie, fie! pah, pah!

> Give me an ounce of civet, good apothecary, to sweeten my imagination.

> There's money for thee.

李尔：　　嗯，从头到脚都是君王；我只要一瞪眼睛，我的臣子就要吓得发抖。我赦免那个人的死罪。你犯的是什么案子？奸淫吗？你不用死；为了奸淫而犯死罪！不，小鸟儿都在干那把戏，金苍蝇当着我的面也会公然交合哩。让通奸的人多子多孙吧；因为葛罗斯特的私生的儿子，也比我的合法的女儿更孝顺他的父亲。淫风越盛越好，我巴不得他们替我多制造几个兵士出来。瞧那个脸上堆着假笑的妇人，她装出一副守身如玉的神气，做作得那么端庄贞静，一听见人家谈起调情的话儿就要摇头；其实她自己干起那回事来，比臭猫和骚马还要浪得多哩。她们的上半身虽然是女人，下半身却是淫荡的妖怪；腰带以上是属于天神的，腰带以下全是属于魔鬼的：那儿是地狱，那儿是黑暗，那儿是火坑，吐着熊熊的烈焰，发出熏人的恶臭，把一切烧成了灰。啐！啐！啐！呸！呸！好掌柜，给我称一两麝香，让我解解我的想象中的臭气；钱在这儿。

EARL OF GLOSTER.　O, let me kiss that hand!

KING LEAR.　Let me wipe it first; it smells of mortality.

EARL OF GLOSTER.　O ruined piece of nature! This great world

Shall so wear out to naught. Dost thou know me?

KING LEAR.　I remember thine eyes well enough. Dost thou squiny at

me? No, do thy worst, blind Cupid! I'll not love. Readthou this

challenge; mark but the penning of it.

EARL OF GLOSTER.　Were all the letters suns, I could not see one.

EDGAR.　[*Aside.*] I would not take this from report. It is,

And my heart breaks at it.

KING LEAR.　Read.

EARL OF GLOSTER.　What, with the case of eyes?

KING LEAR.　O, ho, are you there with me? No eyes in your head, nor

no money in your purse? Your eyes are in a heavy case, your purse

in a light. Yet you see how this world goes.

EARL OF GLOSTER.　I see it feelingly.

KING LEAR.　What, art mad? A man may see how the world goes

with no eyes. Look with thine ears. See how yond justice rails upon

yond simple thief. Hark in thine ear. Change places and,

handy-dandy, which is the justice, which is the thief? Thou hast

seen a farmer's dog bark at a beggar?

EARL OF GLOSTER.　Ay, sir.

KING LEAR.　And the creature run from the cur? There thou mightst

behold the great image of authority: a dog's obeyed in office.

Thou rascal beadle, hold thy bloody hand!

Why dost thou lash that whore? Strip thine own back.

葛罗斯特：　啊！让我吻一吻那只手！

李尔：　让我先把它揩干净；它上面有一股热烘烘的人气。

葛罗斯特：　啊，毁灭了的生命！这一个广大的世界有一天也会像这样零落得只剩一堆残迹。你认识我吗？

李尔：　我很记得你这双眼睛。你在向我瞟吗？不，盲目的丘匹德，随你使出什么手段来，我是再也不会恋爱的。这是一封挑战书，你拿去读吧，瞧瞧它是怎么写的。

葛罗斯特：　即使每一个字都是一个太阳，我也瞧不见。

爱德伽：　（旁白）要是人家告诉我这样的事，我一定不会相信；可是这样的事是真的，我的心要碎了。

李尔：　读呀。

葛罗斯特：　什么！用眼眶子读吗？

李尔：　啊哈！你原来是这个意思吗？你的头上也没有眼睛，你的袋里也没有银钱吗？你的眼眶子真深，你的钱袋真轻。可是你却看见这世界的丑恶。

葛罗斯特：　我只能捉摸到它的丑恶。

李尔：　什么！你疯了吗？一个人就是没有眼睛，也可以看见这世界的丑恶。用你的耳朵瞧着吧：你没看见那法官怎样痛骂那个卑贱的偷儿吗？侧过你的耳朵来，听我告诉你：让他们两人换了地位，谁还认得出哪个是法官，哪个是偷儿？你见过农夫的一条狗向一个乞丐乱吠吗？

葛罗斯特：　嗯，陛下。

李尔：　你还看见那家伙怎样给那条狗赶走吗？从这一件事情上面，你就可以看到威权的伟大的影子；一条得势的狗，也可以使人家唯命是从。你这可恶的教吏，停住你的残忍的手！为什么你要鞭打那个妓女？向你自己的背上着力抽下去吧；你自己心里

Thou hotly lusts to use her in that kind

For which thou whip'st her. The usurer hangs the cozener.

Through tattered clothes small vices do appear;

Robes and furred gowns hide all. Plate sin with gold,

And the strong lance of justice hurtless breaks;

Arm it in rags, a pygmy's straw does pierce it.

None does offend, none – I say none! I'll able 'em.

Take that of me, my friend, who have the power

To seal th' accuser's lips. Get thee glass eyes

And, like a scurvy politician, seem

To see the things thou dost not. Now, now, now, now!

Pull off my boots. Harder, harder! So.

EDGAR. [*Aside.*] O, matter and impertinency mixed!

Reason, in madness!

KING LEAR. If thou wilt weep my fortunes, take my eyes.

I know thee well enough; thy name is Gloster.

Thou must be patient. We came crying hither;

Thou know'st, the first time that we smell the air

We wawl and cry. I will preach to thee. Mark.

EARL OF GLOSTER. Alack, alack the day!

KING LEAR. When we are born, we cry that we are come

To this great stage of fools. This' a good block.

It were a delicate stratagem to shoe

A troop of horse with felt. I'll put't in proof,

And when I have stolen upon these sons-in-law,

Then kill, kill, kill, kill, kill, kill!

和她犯奸淫，却因为她跟人家犯奸淫而鞭打她。那放高利贷的家伙却把那骗子判了死刑。褴褛的衣衫遮不住小小的过失；披上锦袍裘服，便可以隐匿一切。罪恶镀了金，公道的坚强的枪刺戳在上面也会折断；把它用破烂的布条裹起来，一根侏儒的稻草就可以戳破它。没有一个人是犯罪的，我说，没有一个人；我愿意为他们担保；相信我吧，我的朋友，我有权力封住控诉者的嘴唇。你还是去装上一副玻璃眼睛，像一个卑鄙的阴谋家似的，假装能够看见你所看不见的事情吧。来，来，来，来，替我把靴子脱下来；用力一点，用力一点；好。

爱德伽：　（旁白）啊！疯话和正经话夹杂在一起；虽然他发了疯，他说出来的话却不是全无意义的。

李尔：　要是你愿意为我的命运痛哭，那么把我的眼睛拿了去吧。我知道你是什么人；你的名字是葛罗斯特。你必须忍耐；你知道我们来到这世上，第一次嗅到了空气，就哇呀哇呀地哭起来。让我讲一番道理给你听；你听着。

葛罗斯特：　唉！唉！

李尔：　当我们生下地来的时候，我们因为来到了这个全是些傻瓜的广大的舞台之上，所以禁不住放声大哭。这顶帽子的式样很不错！用毡呢钉在一队马儿的蹄上，倒是一个妙计；我要把它实行一下，悄悄地偷进我那两个女婿的营里，然后我就杀呀，杀呀，杀呀，杀呀，杀呀，杀呀！

[*Enter a Gentleman with Attendants.*]

GENTLEMAN.   O, here he is! Lay hand upon him. – Sir,

　　Your most dear daughter –

KING LEAR.   No rescue? What, a prisoner? I am even

　　The natural fool of fortune. Use me well;

　　You shall have ransom. Let me have a surgeon;

　　I am cut to th' brains.

GENTLEMAN.   You shall have anything.

KING LEAR.   No seconds? All myself?

　　Why, this would make a man a man of salt,

　　To use his eyes for garden water-pots,

　　Ay, and laying autumn's dust.

GENTLEMAN.   Good sir-

KING LEAR.   I will die bravely, like a smug bridegroom. What!

　　I will be jovial. Come, come, I am a king;

　　My masters, know you that?

GENTLEMAN.   You are a royal one, and we obey you.

KING LEAR.   Then there's life in't. Nay, an you get it, you shall get it

　　by running. Sa, sa, sa, sa!

　　[*Exit running. Attendants follow.*]

GENTLEMAN.   A sight most pitiful in the meanest wretch,

　　Past speaking of in a king! Thou hast one daughter

　　Who redeems nature from the general curse

　　Which twain have brought her to.

（侍臣率侍从数人上。）

侍臣：　啊！他在这儿；抓住他。陛下，您的最亲爱的女儿——

李尔：　没有人救我吗？什么！我变成一个囚犯了吗？我是天生下来被命运愚弄的。不要虐待我；有人会拿钱来赎我的。替我请几个外科医生来，我的头脑受了伤啦。

侍臣：　您将会得到您所需要的一切。

李尔：　一个伙伴也没有？只有我一个人吗？哎哟，这样会叫一个人变成了个泪人儿，用他的眼睛充作灌园的水壶，去浇洒秋天的泥土。

侍臣：　陛下——

李尔：　我要像一个新郎似的勇敢地死去。嘿！我要高高兴兴的。来，来，我是一个国王，你们知道吗？

侍臣：　您是一位尊严的王上，我们服从您的旨意。

李尔：　那么还有几分希望。要去快去。唦唦唦唦。（下。侍从等随下。）

侍臣：　最微贱的平民到了这样一个地步，也会叫人看了伤心，何况是一个国王！你那两个不孝的女儿，已经使天道人伦受到诅咒，可是你还有一个女儿，却已经把天道人伦从这样的诅咒中间拯救出来了。

EDGAR.   Hail, gentle sir.

GENTLEMAN.   Sir, speed you. What's your will?

EDGAR.   Do you hear aught, sir, of a battle toward?

GENTLEMAN.   Most sure and vulgar. Every one hears that

    Which can distinguish sound.

EDGAR.   But, by your favour, How near's the other army?

GENTLEMAN.   Near and on speedy foot. The main descry

    Stands on the hourly thought.

EDGAR.   I thank you sir. That's all.

GENTLEMAN.   Though that the

    Queen on special cause is here,

    Her army is moved on.

EDGAR.   I thank you, sir

    [*Exit Gentleman.*]

EARL OF GLOSTER.   You ever-gentle gods, take my breath from me;

    Let not my worser spirit tempt me again

    To die before you please!

EDGAR.   Well pray you, father.

EARL OF GLOSTER.   Now, good sir, what are you?

EDGAR.   A most poor man, made tame to fortune's blows,

    Who, by the art of known and feeling sorrows,

    Am pregnant to good pity. Give me your hand;

    I'll lead you to some biding.

EARL OF GLOSTER.   Hearty thanks.

    The bounty and the benison of heaven

    To boot, and boot!

爱德伽：　　祝福，先生。

侍臣：　　足下有什么见教？

爱德伽：　　您有没有听见什么关于将要发生一场战事的消息？

侍臣：　　这已经是一件千真万确、谁都知道的事了；每一个耳朵能
　　　　　够辨别声音的人都听到过那样的消息。

爱德伽：　　可是借问一声，您知道对方的军队离这儿还有多少路？

侍臣：　　很近了，他们一路来得很快；他们的主力部队每一点钟都
　　　　　有到来的可能。

爱德伽：　　谢谢您，先生；这是我所要知道的一切。

侍臣：　　王后虽然有特别的原因还在这儿，她的军队已经开上去了。

爱德伽：　　谢谢您，先生。（侍臣下。）

葛罗斯特：　　永远仁慈的神明，请停止我的呼吸吧；不要在你没有
　　　　　要我离开人世之前，再让我的罪恶的灵魂引诱我结束我自己的
　　　　　生命！

爱德伽：　　您祷告得很好，老人家。

葛罗斯特：　　好先生，您是什么人？

爱德伽：　　一个非常穷苦的人，受惯命运的打击；因为自己是从忧
　　　　　患中间过来的，所以对于不幸的人很容易抱同情。把您的手给
　　　　　我，让我把您领到一处可以栖身的地方去。

葛罗斯特：　　多谢多谢；愿上天大大赐福给您！

[*Enter Oswald.*]

OSWALD.   A proclaimed prize! Most happy!

    That eyeless head of thine was first framed flesh

    To raise my fortunes. Thou old unhappy traitor,

    Briefly thyself remember. The sword is out

    That must destroy thee.

EARL OF GLOSTER.   Now let thy friendly hand

    Put strength enough to't.

    [*Edgar interposes.*]

OSWALD.   Wherefore, bold peasant,

    Dar'st thou support a published traitor? Hence!

    Lest that th' infection of his fortune take

    Like hold on thee. Let go his arm.

EDGAR.   Chill not let go, zir, without vurther casion.

OSWALD.   Let go, slave, or thou diest!

EDGAR.   Good gentleman, go your gait, and let poor voke pass. An chud ha bin zwaggered out of my life, 'twould not ha' bin zo long as 'tis by a vortnight. Nay, come not near th' old man. Keep out, che vor ye, or Ise try whether your costard or my bat be the harder. Chill be plain with you.

OSWALD.   Out, dunghill!

    [*They fight.*]

EDGAR.   Chill pick your teeth, zir. Come; no matter vor your foins.

    [*They fight, and Edgar knocks him down.*]

OSWALD.   Slave, thou hast slain me. Villain, take my purse.

（奥斯华德上。）

奥斯华德： 明令缉拿的要犯！好极了，居然碰在我的手里！你那颗瞎眼的头颅，却是我的进身的阶梯。你这倒霉的老奸贼，赶快忏悔你的罪恶。剑已经拔出了，你今天难逃一死。

葛罗斯特： 但愿你这慈悲的手多用一些气力，帮助我早早脱离苦痛。（爱德伽劝阻奥斯华德。）

奥斯华德： 大胆的村夫，你怎么敢袒护一个明令缉拿的叛徒？滚开，免得你也遭到和他同样的命运。放开他的胳臂。

爱德伽： 先生，你不向我说明理由，我是不放的。

奥斯华德： 放开，奴才，否则我叫你死。

爱德伽： 好先生，你走你的路，让穷人们过去吧。要是这种吓人的话也能把我吓倒，那么我早在半个月之前，就给人吓死了。不，不要走近这个老头儿；我关照你，走远一点儿；要不然的话，我要试一试究竟还是你的头硬还是我的棍子硬。我可不知道什么客气不客气。

奥斯华德： 走开，混账东西！（二人决斗。）

爱德伽： 我要拔掉你的牙齿，先生。来，尽管刺过来吧。（爱德伽击奥斯华德倒地。）

奥斯华德： 奴才，你打死我了。把我的钱囊拿了去吧。要是你希

If ever thou wilt thrive, bury my body,

And give the letters which thou find'st about me

To Edmund Earl of Gloster. Seek him out

Upon the British party. O, untimely death!

Death!

[*He dies.*]

EDGAR.   I know thee well. A serviceable villain,

As duteous to the vices of thy mistress

As badness would desire.

EARL OF GLOSTER.   What, is he dead?

EDGAR.   Sit you down, father; rest you.

Let's see his pockets; these letters that he speaks of

May be my friends.

He's dead. I am only sorry

He had no other deathsman. Let us see.

Leave, gentle wax; and, manners, blame us not.

To know our enemies' minds, we'ld rip their hearts;

Their papers, is more lawful.

[*Reads.*] Let our reciprocal vows be rememb'red. You have many opportunities to cut him off. If your will want not, time and place will be fruitfully offered. There is nothing done, if he return the conqueror. Then am I the prisoner, and his bed my jail; from the loathed warmth whereof deliver me, and supply the place for your labour. Your – wife, so I would say   – affectionate servant,

Goneril.

望将来有好日子过，请你把我的尸体掘一个坑埋了；我身边还有一封信，请你替我送给葛罗斯特伯爵爱德蒙大爷，他在英国军队里，你可以找到他。啊！想不到我死于非命！（死。）

爱德伽：　我认识你；你是一个惯会讨主上欢心的奴才；你的女主人无论有什么万恶的命令，你总是奉命唯谨。

葛罗斯特：　什么！他死了吗？

爱德伽：　坐下来，老人家；您休息一会儿吧。让我们搜一搜他的衣袋——他说起的这一封信，也许可以对我有一点用处。他死了；我只可惜他不是死在刽子手的手里。让我们看：对不起，好蜡，我要把你拆开来了；恕我无礼，为了要知道我们敌人的居心，就是他们的心肝也要剖出来，拆阅他们的信件不算是违法的事。"不要忘记我们彼此间的誓约。你有许多机会可以除去他；只要你有决心，一切都是不成问题的。要是他得胜归来，那就什么都完了；我将要成为一个囚人，他的眠床就是我的牢狱。把我从他可憎的怀抱中拯救出来吧，他的地位你可以取而代之，这也是你应得的酬劳。你的恋慕的奴婢——但愿我能换上妻子两个字——高纳里尔。"啊，不可测度的女人的心！谋害她的善良的丈夫，叫我的兄弟代替他的位置！在这砂土之内，我要把你掩埋起来，你这杀人的淫妇的使者。在一个适当的时间，我要让那被人阴谋弑害的公爵见到这一封卑劣的信。我能够把你的死讯和你的使命告诉他，对于他是一件幸运的事。

O undistinguished space of woman's will!

A plot upon her virtuous husband's life,

And the exchange my brother! Here in the sands

Thee I'll rake up, the post unsanctified

Of murderous lechers; and in the mature time

With this ungracious paper strike the sight

Of the death-practised Duke, For him 'tis well

That of thy death and business I can tell.

EARL OF GLOSTER.   The King is mad. How stiff is my vile sense,

That I stand up, and have ingenious feeling

Of my huge sorrows! Better I were distract:

And woes by wrong imaginations lose

The knowledge of themselves.

EDGAR.   Give me your hand.

[*A drum afar off.*]

Far off methinks I hear the beaten drum.

Come, father, I'll bestow you with a friend.

[*Exeunt.*]

葛罗斯特：　王上疯了；我的万恶的知觉却是倔强得很，我一站起身来，无限的悲痛就涌上我的心头！还是疯了的好；那样我可以不再想到我的不幸，让一切痛苦在昏乱的幻想之中忘记了它们本身的存在。

爱德伽：　把您的手给我；（远处鼓声。）好像我听见远远有打鼓的声音。来，老人家，让我把您安顿在一个朋友的地方。（同下。）

ACT IV　SCENE VII

A tent in the French camp.

[*Enter Cordelia, Kent, Doctor, and Gentleman.*]

CORDELIA.　O thou good Kent, how shall I live and work

　　To match thy goodness? My life will be too short

　　And every measure fail me.

EARL OF KENT.　To be acknowledged, madam, is o'er-paid.

　　All my reports go with the modest truth;

　　Nor more nor clipped, but so.

CORDELIA.　Be better suited.

　　These weeds are memories of those worser hours.

　　I prithee put them off.

EARL OF KENT.　Pardon, dear madam.

　　Yet to be known shortens my made intent.

　　My boon I make it that you know me not

　　Till time and I think meet.

CORDELIA.　Then be't so, my good lord.

　　[*To the Doctor.*] How, does the King?

DOCTOR.　Madam, sleeps still.

CORDELIA.　O you kind gods,

　　Cure this great breach in his abused nature!

第四幕　第七场

法军营帐。
（考狄利娅、肯特、医生及侍臣上。）

考狄利娅：　好肯特啊！我怎么能够报答你这一番苦心好意呢！就是粉身碎骨，也不能抵偿你的大德。

肯特：　娘娘，只要自己的苦心被人了解，那就是莫大的报酬了。我所讲的话，句句都是事实，没有一分增减。

考狄利娅：　去换一身好一点的衣服吧；您身上的衣服是那一段悲惨的时光中的纪念品，请你脱下来吧。

肯特：　恕我，娘娘；我现在还不能回复我的本来面目，因为那会妨碍我的预定的计划。请您准许我这一个要求，在我自己认为还没有到适当的时间以前，您必须把我当做一个不相识的人。

考狄利娅：　那么就照你的意思吧，伯爵。（向医生）王上怎样？

医生：　娘娘，他仍旧睡着。

考狄利娅：　慈悲的神明啊，医治他的被凌辱的心灵中的重大的裂痕！保佑这一个被不孝的女儿所反噬的老父，让他错乱昏迷的

Th' untuned and jarring senses, O, wind up

Of this child-changed father!

DOCTOR.   So please your Majesty

That we may wake the King? He hath slept long

CORDELIA.   Be governed by your knowledge, and proceed

I' th' sway of your own will. Is he arrayed?

[*Enter Lear in a chair carried by Servants.*]

GENTLEMAN.   Ay, madam. In the heaviness of sleep

We put fresh garments on him.

DOCTOR.   Be by, good madam, when we do awake him.

I doubt not of his temperance.

CORDELIA.   Very well.

[*Music.*]

DOCTOR.   Please you draw near. Louder the music there!

CORDELIA.   O my dear father, restoration hang

Thy medicine on my lips, and let this kiss

Repair those violent harms that my two sisters

Have in thy reverence made!

EARL OF KENT.   Kind and dear princess!

CORDELIA.   Had you not been their father, these white flakes

Had challenged pity of them. Was this a face

To be opposed against the warring winds?

To stand against the deep dread-bolted thunder?

神智回复健全吧！

医生：　　请问娘娘，我们现在可不可以叫王上醒来？他已经睡得很久了。

考狄利娅：　　照你的意见，应该怎么办就怎么办吧。他有没有穿着好？

（李尔卧椅内，众仆舁上。）

侍臣：　　是，娘娘；我们乘着他熟睡的时候，已经替他把新衣服穿上去了。

医生：　　娘娘，请您不要走开，等我们叫他醒来；我相信他的神经已经安定下来了。

考狄利娅：　　很好。（乐声。）

医生：　　请您走近一步。音乐还要响一点儿。

考狄利娅：　　啊，我的亲爱的父亲！但愿我的嘴唇上有治愈疯狂的灵药，让这一吻抹去了我那两个姐姐加在你身上的无情的伤害吧！

肯特：　　善良的好公主！

考狄利娅：　　假如你不是她们的父亲，这满头的白雪也该引起她们的怜悯。这样一张面庞是受得起激战的狂风吹打的吗？它能够抵御可怕的雷霆吗？在最惊人的闪电的光辉之下，你，可怜的无援的兵士！戴着这一顶薄薄的戎盔，苦苦地守住你的哨岗

In the most terrible and nimble stroke

Of quick cross lightning? to watch – poor perdu! –

With this thin helm? Mine enemy's dog,

Though he had bit me, should have stood that night

Against my fire; and wast thou fain, poor father,

To hovel thee with swine and rogues forlorn,

In short and musty straw? Alack, alack!

'Tis wonder that thy life and wits at once

Had not concluded all. – He wakes. Speak to him.

DOCTOR.　Madam, do you; 'tis fittest.

CORDELIA.　How does my royal lord? How fares your Majesty?

KING LEAR.　You do me wrong to take me out o' th' grave.

Thou art a soul in bliss; but I am bound

Upon a wheel of fire, that mine own tears

Do scald like molten lead.

CORDELIA.　Sir, do you know me?

KING LEAR.　You are a spirit, I know. When did you die?

CORDELIA.　Still, still, far wide!

DOCTOR.　He's scarce awake. Let him alone awhile.

KING LEAR.　Where have I been? Where am I? Fair daylight,

I am mightily abused. I should e'en die with pity,

To see another thus. I know not what to say.

I will not swear these are my hands. Let's see.

I feel this pin prick. Would I were assured

Of my condition!

CORDELIA.　O, look upon me, sir,

吗？我的敌人的狗，即使它曾经咬过我，在那样的夜里，我也要让它躺在我的火炉之前。但是你，可怜的父亲，却甘心钻在污秽霉烂的稻草里，和猪狗、和流浪的乞儿做伴吗？唉！唉！你的生命不和你的智慧同归于尽，才是一件怪事。他醒来了；对他说些什么话吧。

医生：　　娘娘，应该您去跟他说说。

考狄利娅：　父王陛下，您好吗？

李尔：　　你们不应该把我从坟墓中间拖了出来。你是一个有福的灵魂；我却缚在一个烈火的车轮上，我自己的眼泪也像熔铅一样灼痛我的脸。

考狄利娅：　父亲，您认识我吗？

李尔：　　你是一个灵魂，我知道；你在什么时候死的？

考狄利娅：　还是疯疯癫癫的。

医生：　　他还没有完全清醒过来；暂时不要惊扰他。

李尔：　　我到过些什么地方？现在我在什么地方？明亮的白昼吗？我大大受了骗啦。我如果看见别人落到这一个地步，我也要为他心碎而死。我不知道应该怎么说。我不愿发誓这一双是我的手；让我试试看，这针刺上去是觉得痛的。但愿我能够知道我自己的实在情形！

考狄利娅：　啊！瞧着我，父亲，把您的手按在我的头上为我祝福

And hold your hands in benediction o'er me.

No, sir, you must not kneel.

KING LEAR.   Pray, do not mock me.

I am a very foolish fond old man,

Fourscore and upward, not an hour more nor less;

And, to deal plainly,

I fear I am not in my perfect mind.

Methinks I should know you, and know this man;

Yet I am doubtful; for I am mainly ignorant

What place this is; and all the skill I have

Remembers not these garments; nor I know not

Where I did lodge last night. Do not laugh at me;

For as I am a man I think this lady

To be my child Cordelia.

CORDELIA.   And so I am! I am!

KING LEAR.   Be your tears wet? Yes, faith. I pray weep not.

If you have poison for me, I will drink it.

I know you do not love me; for your sisters

Have, as I do remember, done me wrong.

You have some cause, they have not.

CORDELIA.   No cause, no cause.

KING LEAR.   Am I in France?

EARL OF KENT.   In your own kingdom, sir.

KING LEAR.   Do not abuse me.

DOCTOR.   Be comforted, good madam. The great rage

You see is killed in him; and yet it is danger

吧。不，父亲，您千万不能跪下。

李尔： 请不要取笑我；我是一个非常愚蠢的傻老头子，活了八十多岁了；不瞒您说，我怕我的头脑有点儿不大健全。我想我应该认识您，也该认识这个人；可是我不敢确定；因为我全然不知道这是什么地方，而且凭着我所有的能力，我也记不起来什么时候穿上这身衣服；我也不知道昨天晚上我在什么所在过夜。不要笑我；我想这位夫人是我的孩子考狄利娅。

考狄利娅： 正是，正是。

李尔： 你在流着眼泪吗？当真。请你不要哭啦；要是你有毒药为我预备着，我愿意喝下去。我知道你不爱我；因为我记得你的两个姐姐都虐待我；你虐待我还有几分理由，她们却没有理由虐待我。

考狄利娅： 谁都没有这理由。

李尔： 我是在法国吗？

肯特： 在您自己的国土之内，陛下。

李尔： 不要骗我。

医生： 请宽心一点，娘娘；您看他的疯狂已经平静下去了；可是再向他提起他经历的事情，却是非常危险的。不要多烦扰他，

To make him even o'er the time he has lost.

Desire him to go in. Trouble him no more

Till further settling.

CORDELIA.　Will't please your Highness walk?

KING LEAR.　You must bear with me.

Pray you now, forget and forgive. I am old and foolish.

[*Exeunt all but Kent and Gentleman.*]

GENTLEMAN.　Holds it true, sir, that the Duke of Cornwall was so slain?

EARL OF KENT.　Most certain, sir.

GENTLEMAN.　Who is conductor of his people?

EARL OF KENT.　As 'tis said, the bastard son of Gloster.

GENTLEMAN.　They say Edgar, his banished son, is with the Earl of Kent in Germany.

EARL OF KENT.　Report is changeable. 'Tis time to look about; the powers of the kingdom approach apace.

GENTLEMAN.　The arbitrement is like to be bloody. Fare you well, sir.

[*Exit.*]

EARL OF KENT.　My point and period will be throughly wrought,

Or well or ill, as this day's battle's fought.

[*Exit.*]

让他的神经完全安定下来。

考狄利娅：　请陛下到里边去安息安息吧。

李尔：　你必须原谅我。请你不咎既往，宽赦我的过失；我是个年老糊涂的人。（李尔、考狄利娅、医生及侍从等同下。）

侍臣：　先生，康华尔公爵被刺的消息是真的吗？

肯特：　完全真确。

侍臣：　他的军队归什么人带领？

肯特：　据说是葛罗斯特的庶子。

侍臣：　他们说他的放逐在外的儿子爱德伽现在跟肯特伯爵都在德国。

肯特：　消息常常变化不定。现在是应该戒备的时候了，英国军队已在迅速逼近。

侍臣：　一场血战是免不了的。再会，先生。（下。）

肯特：　我的目的能不能顺利达到，要看这一场战事的结果方才分晓。（下。）

ACT V   SCENE I

The British camp, near Dover.
[*Enter, with drum and colours. Edmund, Regan, Officers, Soldiers and others.*]

EDMUND.   [*To an Officer.*] Know of the Duke if his last purpose hold,
    Or whether since he is advised by aught
    To change the course. He's full of alteration
    And self-reproving. Bring his constant pleasure.
    [*Exit an Officer.*]
REGAN.   Our sister's man is certainly miscarried.
EDMUND.   Tis to be doubted, madam.
REGAN.   Now, sweet lord,
    You know the goodness I intend upon you.
    Tell me – but truly – but then speak the truth –
    Do you not love my sister?
EDMUND.   In honoured love.
REGAN.   But have you never found my brother's way
    To the forfended place?
EDMUND.   That thought abuses you.
REGAN.   I am doubtful that you have been conjunct

第五幕　第一场

多佛附近英军营地。

（旗鼓前导。爱德蒙、里根、军官、兵士及侍从等上。）

爱德蒙：　（向一军官）你去问一声公爵，他是不是仍旧保持着原
　　　来的决心，还是因为有了其他的理由，已经改变了方针；他这
　　　个人摇摆不定，畏首畏尾；我要知道他究竟抱着怎样的主张。
　　　（军官下。）

里根：　我那姐姐差来的人一定在路上出了事啦。

爱德蒙：　那可说不定，夫人。

里根：　好爵爷，我对你的一片好心，你不会不知道的；现在请你
　　　告诉我，老老实实地告诉我，你不爱我的姐姐吗？

爱德蒙：　我只是按照我的名分敬爱她。

里根：　可是你从来没有深入我的姐夫的禁地吗？

爱德蒙：　这样的思想是有失您自己的体统的。

里根：　我怕你们已经打成一片，她心坎儿里只有你一个人哩。

And bosomed with her, as far as we call hers.

EDMUND.　No, by mine honour, madam.

REGAN.　I never shall endure her. Dear my lord,

Be not familiar with her.

EDMUND.　Fear me not.

She and the Duke her husband!

[*Enter, with drum and colours, Albany, Goneril, and Soldiers.*]

GONERIL.　[*Aside.*] I had rather lose the battle than that sister

Should loosen him and me.

DUKE OF ALBANY.　Our very loving sister, well be-met.

Sir, this I hear: the King is come to his daughter,

With others whom the rigour of our state

Forced to cry out. Where I could not be honest,

I never yet was valiant. For this business,

It touches us as France invades our land,

Not bolds the King, with others whom, I fear,

Most just and heavy causes make oppose.

EDMUND.　Sir, you speak nobly.

REGAN.　Why is this reasoned?

GONERIL.　Combine together 'gainst the enemy;

For these domestic and particular broils

Are not the question here.

DUKE OF ALBANY.　Let's then determine

With th' ancient of war on our proceeding.

爱德蒙：　　凭着我的名誉起誓，夫人，没有这样的事。

里根：　　我绝不答应她；我的亲爱的爵爷，不要跟她亲热。

爱德蒙：　　您放心吧。——她跟她的公爵丈夫来啦！

（旗鼓前导，奥本尼、高纳里尔及兵士等上。）

高纳里尔：　　（旁白）我宁愿这一次战争失败，也不让我那个妹子
　　　　把他从我手里夺了去。

奥本尼：　　贤妹久违了。伯爵，我听说王上已经带了一班受不住我
　　　　国的苛政、高呼不平的人们，到他女儿的地方去了。要是我们
　　　　所兴的是一场不义之师，我是再也提不起我的勇气来的；可是
　　　　现在的问题，并不是我们的王上和他手下的一群人在法国的煽
　　　　动之下，用堂堂正正的理由向我们兴师问罪，而是法国举兵侵
　　　　犯我们的领土，这是我们所不能容忍的。

爱德蒙：　　您说得有理，佩服，佩服。

里根：　　这种话讲它做什么呢？

高纳里尔：　　我们只需同心合力，打退敌人；这些内部的纠纷，不
　　　　是现在所要讨论的问题。

奥本尼：　　那么让我们跟那些久历戎行的战士们讨论讨论我们所应
　　　　该采取的战略吧。

EDMUND. I shall attend you presently at your tent.

REGAN. Sister, you'll go with us?

GONERIL. No.

REGAN. 'Tis most convenient. Pray you go with us.

GONERIL. [*Aside.*] O, ho, I know the riddle. –

　　I will go.

[*Enter Edgar disguised.*]

EDGAR. If e'er your Grace had speech with man so poor,

　　Hear me one word.

DUKE OF ALBANY. I'll overtake you. – Speak.

　　[*Exeunt all but Albany and Edgar.*]

EDGAR. Before you fight the battle, ope this letter.

　　If you have victory, let the trumpet sound

　　For him that brought it. Wretched though I seem,

　　I can produce a champion that will prove

　　What is avouched there. If you miscarry,

　　Your business of the world hath so an end,

　　And machination ceases. Fortune love you!

DUKE OF ALBANY. Stay till I have read the letter.

EDGAR. I was forbid it.

　　When time shall serve, let but the herald cry,

　　And I'll appear again.

DUKE OF ALBANY. Why, fare thee well. I will o'erlook thy paper.

　　[*Exit Edgar.*]

爱德蒙：　　很好，我就到您的帐里来叨陪末议。

里根：　　姐姐，您也跟我们一块儿去吗？

高纳里尔：　　不。

里根：　　您怎么可以不去？来，请吧。

高纳里尔：　　（旁白）哼！我明白你的意里。好，我就去。

（爱德伽乔装上。）

爱德伽：　　殿下要是不嫌我微贱，请听我说一句话。

奥本尼：　　你们先请一步，我就来。——说。（爱德蒙、里根、高纳里尔、军官、兵士及侍从等同下。）

爱德伽：　　在您没有开始作战以前，先把这封信拆开来看一看。要是您得到胜利，可以吹喇叭为信号，叫我出来；虽然您看我是这样一个下贱的人，我可以请出一个证人来，证明这信上所写的事。要是您失败了，那么您在这世上的使命已经完毕，一切阴谋也都无能为力了。愿命运眷顾您！

奥本尼：　　等我读了信你再去。

爱德伽：　　我不能。时候一到，您只要叫传令官传唤一声，我就会出来的。

奥本尼：　　那么再见；你的信我拿回去看吧。（爱德伽下。）

[*Enter Edmund.*]

EDMUND.　　The enemy 's in view; draw up your powers.

　　　　Here is the guess of their true strength and forces

　　　　By diligent discovery; but your haste

　　　　Is now urged on you.

DUKE OF ALBANY.　　We will greet the time.

　　　　[*Exit.*]

EDMUND.　　To both these sisters have I sworn my love;

　　　　Each jealous of the other, as the stung

　　　　Are of the adder. Which of them shall I take?

　　　　Both? one? or neither? Neither can be enjoyed,

　　　　If both remain alive. To take the widow

　　　　Exasperates, makes mad her sister Goneril;

　　　　And hardly shall I carry out my side,

　　　　Her husband being alive. Now then, we'll use

　　　　His countenance for the battle, which being done,

　　　　Let her who would be rid of him devise

　　　　His speedy taking off. As for the mercy

　　　　Which he intends to Lear and to Cordelia –

　　　　The battle done, and they within our power,

　　　　Shall never see his pardon; for my state

　　　　Stands on me to defend, not to debate.

　　　　[*Exit.*]

（爱德蒙重上。）

爱德蒙：　　敌人已经望得见了；快把您的军队集合起来。这儿记载着根据精密侦查所得的敌方军力的估计；可是现在您必须快点儿了。

奥本尼：　　好，我们准备迎敌就是了。（下。）

爱德蒙：　　我对这两个姐姐都已经立下爱情的盟誓；她们彼此互怀嫉妒，就像被蛇咬过的人见不得蛇的影子一样。我应该选择哪一个呢？两个都要？只要一个？还是一个也不要？要是两个全都留在世上，我就一个也不能到手；娶了那寡妇，一定会激怒她的姐姐高纳里尔；可是她的丈夫一天不死，我又怎么能跟她成双配对？现在我们还是要借他做号召军心的幌子；等到战事结束以后，她要是想除去他，让她自己设法结果他的性命吧。照他的意思，李尔和考狄利娅两人被我们捉到以后，是不能加害的；可是假如他们果然落在我们手里，我们可绝不让他们得到他的赦免；因为我保全自己的地位要紧，什么天理良心只好一概不论。（下。）

ACT V   SCENE II

A field between the two camps.

[Alarum within. Enter, with drum and colours, Lear, Cordelia and their Forces over the stage; and exeunt. Enter Edgar and Gloster.]

EDGAR.   Here, father, take the shadow of this tree
    For your good host. Pray that the right may thrive.
    If ever I return to you again,
    I'll bring you comfort.
EARL OF GLOSTER.   Grace go with you, sir!
    [Exit Edgar.]

[Alarum and retreat within. Enter Edgar.]

EDGAR.   Away, old man! give me thy hand! away!
    King Lear hath lost, he and his daughter ta'en.
    Give me thy hand! come on!
EARL OF GLOSTER.   No further, sir. A man may rot even here.
EDGAR.   What, in ill thoughts again? Men must endure
    Their going hence, even as their coming hither;
    Ripeness is all. Come on.
EARL OF GLOSTER.   And that's true too.
    [Exeunt.]

第五幕　第二场

两军营地之间的原野。

（内号角声。旗鼓前导，李尔及考狄利娅率军队上；同下。爱德伽
及葛罗斯特上。）

爱德伽：　来，老人家，在这树荫底下坐坐吧；但愿正义得到胜利！
　　　要是我还能够回来见您，我一定会给您好消息的。

葛罗斯特：　上帝照顾您，先生！（爱德伽下。）

（号角声；有顷，内吹退军号。爱德伽重上。）

爱德伽：　去吧，老人家！把您的手给我；去吧！李尔王已经失败，
　　　他跟他的女儿都被他们捉去了。把您的手给我；来。

葛罗斯特：　不，先生，我不想再到什么地方去了；让我就在这儿
　　　等死吧。

爱德伽：　怎么！您又转起那种坏念头来了吗？人们的生死都不是
　　　可以勉强求到的，你应该耐心忍受天命的安排。来。

葛罗斯特：　那也说得有理。（同下。）

ACT V   SCENE III

The British camp, near Dover.

[Enter, in conquest, with drum and colours, Edmund; Lear and Cordelia
as prisoners; Officers, Soldiers, & c.]

EDMUND.   Some officers take them away. Good guard

Until their greater pleasures first be known

That are to censure them.

CORDELIA.   We are not the first

Who with best meaning have incurred the worst.

For thee, oppressèd king, am I cast down;

Myself could else outfrown false Fortune's frown.

Shall we not see these daughters and these sisters?

KING LEAR.   No, no, no, no! Come, let's away to prison.

We two alone will sing like birds i' th' cage.

When thou dost ask me blessing, I'll kneel down

And ask of thee forgiveness. So we'll live,

And pray, and sing, and tell old tales, and laugh

At gilded butterflies, and hear poor rogues

Talk of court news; and we'll talk with them too –

Who loses and who wins; who's in, who's out –

And take upon 's the mystery of things,

第五幕　第三场

多佛附近英军营地。

（旗鼓前导，爱德蒙凯旋上；李尔、考狄利娅被俘随上；军官、兵士等同上。）

爱德蒙：　来人，把他们押下去，好生看守，等上面发落下来，再作道理。

考狄利娅：　存心良善的反而得到恶报，这样的前例是很多的。我只是为了你，被迫害的国王，才感到悲伤；否则尽管欺人的命运向我横眉怒目，我也不把她的凌辱放在心上。我们要不要去见见这两个女儿和这两个姐姐？

李尔：　不，不，不，不！来，让我们到监牢里去。我们两人将要像笼中之鸟一般唱歌；当你求我为你祝福的时候，我要跪下来求你饶恕；我们就这样生活着，祈祷，唱歌，说些古老的故事，嘲笑那班像金翅蝴蝶般的廷臣，听听那些可怜的人们讲些宫廷里的消息；我们也要跟他们在一起谈话，谁失败，谁胜利，谁在朝，谁在野，用我们的意见解释各种事情的奥秘，就像我们是上帝的耳目一样；在囚牢的四壁之内，我们将要冷眼看那些朋比为奸的党徒随着月亮的圆缺而升沉。

As if we were God's spies; and we'll wear out,

In a walled prison, packs and sects of great ones

That ebb and flow by th' moon.

EDMUND.　　Take them away.

KING LEAR.　　Upon such sacrifices, my Cordelia,

The gods themselves throw incense. Have I caught thee?

He that parts us shall bring a brand from heaven

And fire us hence like foxes. Wipe thine eyes.

The good-years shall devour 'em, flesh and fell,

Ere they shall make us weep! We'll see 'em starved first.

Come.

[*Exeunt Lear and Cordelia, guarded.*]

EDMUND.　　Come hither, Captain; hark.

Take thou this note. [*Giving a paper.*]

Go follow them to prison.

One step I have advanced thee. If thou dost

As this instructs thee, thou dost make thy way

To noble fortunes. Know thou this, that men

Are as the time is. To be tender-minded

Does not become a sword. Thy great employment

Will not bear question. Either say thou'lt do't,

Or thrive by other means.

OFFICER.　　I'll do't, my lord.

EDMUND.　　About it! and write happy when th' hast done.

Mark – I say, instantly; and carry it so

爱德蒙：　　把他们带下去。

李尔：　　对于这样的祭物，我的考狄利娅，天神也要焚香致敬的。我果然把你捉住了吗？谁要是想分开我们，必须从天上取下一把火炬来像驱逐狐狸一样把我们赶散。揩干你的眼睛；让恶疮烂掉他们的全身，他们也不能使我们流泪，我们要看他们活活饿死。来。（兵士押李尔、考狄利娅下。）

爱德蒙：　　过来，队长。听着，把这一通密令拿去；（以一纸授军官。）跟着他们到监牢里去。我已经把你提升了一级，要是你能够照这密令上所说的执行，一定大有好处。你要知道，识时务的才是好汉；心肠太软的人不配佩带刀剑。我吩咐你去干这件重要的差使，你可不必多问，愿意就做，不愿意就另谋出路吧。

军官：　　我愿意，大人。

爱德蒙：　　那么去吧；你立了这一个功劳，你就是一个幸运的人。听着，事不宜迟，必须照我所写的办法赶快办好。

As I have set it down.

OFFICER.　　I cannot draw a cart, nor eat dried oats;

If it be man's work, I'll do't.

[*Exit.*]

[*Flourish. Enter Albany, Goneril, Regan, Officers, and Attendants.*]

DUKE OF ALBANY.　　Sir, you have showed to-day your valiant strain,

And fortune led you well. You have the captives

Who were the opposites of this day's strife.

We do require them of you, so to use them

As we shall find their merits and our safety

May equally determine.

EDMUND.　　Sir, I thought it fit

To send the old and miserable King

To some retention and appointed guard;

Whose age has charms in it, whose title more,

To pluck the common bosom on his side

And turn our impressed lances in our eyes

Which do command them. With him I sent the Queen,

My reason all the same; and they are ready

To-morrow, or at further space, t' appear

Where you shall hold your session. At this time

We sweat and bleed: the friend hath lost his friend;

And the best quarrels, in the heat, are cursed

军官：　我不会拖车子，也不会吃干麦；只要是男子汉干的事，我就会干。（下。）

（喇叭奏花腔。奥本尼、高纳里尔、里根、军官及侍从等上。）

奥本尼：　伯爵，你今天果然表明了你是一个将门之子；命运眷顾着你，使你克奏朕功，跟我们敌对的人都已经束手就擒。请你把你的俘虏交给我们，让我们一方面按照他们的身份，一方面顾到我们自身的安全，决定一个适当的处置。

爱德蒙：　殿下，我已经把那不幸的老王拘禁起来，并且派兵严密监视了；我认为应该这样办；他的高龄和尊号都有一种莫大的魔力，可以吸引人心归附他，要是不加防范，恐怕我们的部下都要受他的煽惑而对我们反戈相向。那王后我为了同样的理由，也把她一起下了监；他们明天或者迟一两天就可以受你们的审判。现在弟兄们刚刚流过血汗，丧折了不少的朋友亲人，他们感受战争的残酷，未免心中愤激，这场争端无论理由怎样正大，在他们看来也就成为是可诅咒的了；所以审问考狄利娅和她的父亲这一件事，必须在一个更适当的时候举行。

By those that feel their sharpness.

The question of Cordelia and her father.

Requires a fitter place.

DUKE OF ALBANY.   Sir, by your patience,

I hold you but a subject of this war,

Not as a brother.

REGAN.   That's as we list to grace him.

Methinks our pleasure might have been demanded

Ere you had spoke so far. He led our powers,

Bore the commission of my place and person,

The which immediacy may well stand up

And call itself your brother.

GONERIL.   Not so hot!

In his own grace he doth exalt himself

More than in your addition.

REGAN.   In my rights

By me invested, he compeers the best.

GONERIL.   That were the most if he should husband you.

REGAN.   Jesters do oft prove prophets.

GONERIL.   Holla, holla!

That eye that told you so looked but asquint.

REGAN.   Lady, I am not well; else I should answer

From a full-flowing stomach. General,

Take thou my soldiers, prisoners, patrimony;

Dispose of them, of me; the walls are thine.

Witness the world that I create thee here

奥本尼： 伯爵，说一句不怕你见怪的话，你不过是一个随征的将领，我并没有把你当做一个同等地位的人。

里根： 假如我愿意，为什么他不能和你分庭抗礼呢？我想你在说这样的话以前，应该先问问我的意思才是。他带领我们的军队，受到我的全权委任，凭着这一层亲密的关系，也够资格和你称兄道弟了。

高纳里尔： 少亲热点儿吧；他的地位是他靠着自己的才能造成的，并不是你给他的恩典。

里根： 我把我的权力托付给他，他就能和最尊贵的人匹敌。

高纳里尔： 要是他做了你的丈夫，至多也不过如此吧。

里根： 笑话往往会变成预言。

高纳里尔： 呵呵！看你挤眉弄眼的，果然有点儿邪气。

里根： 太太，我现在身子不大舒服，懒得跟你斗口了。将军，请你接受我的军队、俘虏和财产；这一切连我自己都由你支配；我是你的献城降服的臣仆；让全世界为我证明，我现在把你立为我的丈夫和君主。

My lord and master.

GONERIL.　　Mean you to enjoy him?

DUKE OF ALBANY.　　The let-alone lies not in your good will.

EDMUND.　　Nor in thine, lord.

DUKE OF ALBANY.　　Half-blooded fellow, yes.

REGAN.　　[*To Edmund.*] Let the drum strike, and prove my title thine.

DUKE OF ALBANY.　　Stay yet; hear reason.

Edmund, I arrest thee On capital treason; and, in thine attaint,

This gilded serpent.

[*Points to Goneril.*]

For your claim, fair sister,

I bar it in the interest of my wife.

’Tis she is subcontracted to this lord,

And I, her husband, contradict your banes.

If you will marry, make your loves to me;

My lady is bespoke.

GONERIL.　　An interlude!

DUKE OF ALBANY.　　Thou art armed, Gloster. Let the trumpet sound.

If none appear to prove upon thy person

Thy heinous, manifest, and many treasons,

There is my pledge. [*Throwing down a glove.*]

I’ll prove it on thy heart,

Ere I taste bread, thou art in nothing less

Than I have here proclaimed thee.

REGAN.　　Sick, O, sick!

GONERIL.　　[*Aside.*] If not, I’ll ne’er trust medicine.

高纳里尔： 你想要受用他吗？

奥本尼： 那不是你所能阻止的。

爱德蒙： 也不是你所能阻止的。

奥本尼： 杂种，我可以阻止你们。

里根： （向爱德蒙）叫鼓手打起鼓来，和他决斗，证明我已经把尊位给了你。

奥本尼： 等一等，我还有话说。爱德蒙，你犯有叛逆重罪，我逮捕你；同时我还要逮捕这一条金鳞的毒蛇。（指高纳里尔）贤妹，为了我的妻子的缘故，我必须要求您放弃您的权利；她已经跟这位勋爵有约在先，所以我，她的丈夫，不得不对你们的婚姻表示异议。要是您想结婚的话，还是把您的爱情用在我的身上吧，我的妻子已经另有所属了。

高纳里尔： 这一段穿插真有趣！

奥本尼： 葛罗斯特，你现在甲胄在身；让喇叭吹起来；要是没有人出来证明你所犯的无数凶残罪恶，众目昭彰的叛逆重罪，这儿是我的信物；（掷下手套。）在我没有剖开你的胸口，证明我此刻所宣布的一切以前，我绝不让一些食物接触我的嘴唇。

里根： 哎哟！我病了！我病了！

高纳里尔： （旁白）要是你不病，我也从此不相信毒药了。

EDMUND.　There's my exchange. [*Throwing down a glove.*]

　　What in the world he is

　　That names me traitor, villain-like he lies.

　　Call by thy trumpet. He that dares approach,

　　On him, on you, who not? I will maintain

　　My truth and honour firmly.

DUKE OF ALBANY.　A herald, ho!

EDMUND.　A herald, ho, a herald!

DUKE OF ALBANY.　Trust to thy single virtue; for thy soldiers,

　　All levied in my name, have in my name

　　Took their discharge.

REGAN.　My sickness grows upon me.

DUKE OF ALBANY.　She is not well. Convey her to my tent.

　　[*Exit Regan, led.*]

[*Enter a Herald.*]

DUKE OF ALBANY.　Come hither, herald. Let the trumpet sound,

　　And read out this.

OFFICER.　Sound, trumpet!

　　[*A trumpet sounds.*]

HERALD.　[*Reads.*] If any man of quality or degree within the lists of the army will maintain upon Edmund, supposed Earl of Gloster, that he is a manifold traitor, let him appear by the third sound of the trumpet. He is bold in his defence.

爱德蒙：　这儿是我给你的交换品；（掷下手套。）谁骂我是叛徒的，他就是个说谎的恶人。叫你的喇叭吹起来吧；谁有胆量，出来，我可以向他、向你、向每一个人证明我的不可动摇的忠心和荣誉。

奥本尼：　来，传令官！

爱德蒙：　传令官！传令官！

奥本尼：　信赖你个人的勇气吧；因为你的军队都是用我的名义征集的，我已经用我的名义把他们遣散了。

里根：　我的病越来越厉害啦！

奥本尼：　她身体不舒服；把她扶到我的帐里去。（侍从扶里根下。）

（传令官上。）

奥本尼：　过来，传令官。叫喇叭吹起来。宣读这一道命令。

军官：　吹喇叭！（喇叭吹响。）

传令官：　（宣读）"在本军之中，如有身份高贵的将校官佐，愿意证明爱德蒙——名分未定的葛罗斯特伯爵，是一个罪恶多端的叛徒，让他在第三次喇叭声中出来。该爱德蒙坚决自卫。"

EDMUND.   Sound.

　　[*First trumpet.*]

HERALD.   Again!

　　[*Second trumpet.*]

　　Again!

　　[*Third trumpet.*]

　　[*Trumpet answers within.*]

[*Enter Edgar, armed, at the third sound, a trumpet before him.*]

DUKE OF ALBANY.   Ask him his purposes, why he appears

　　Upon this call o' th' trumpet.

HERALD.   What are you?

　　Your name, your quality? and why you answer

　　This present summons?

EDGAR.   Know my name is lost;

　　By treason's tooth bare-gnawn and canker-bit.

　　Yet am I noble as the adversary

　　I come to cope.

DUKE OF ALBANY.   Which is that adversary?

EDGAR.   What's he that speaks for Edmund Earl of Gloster?

EDMUND.   Himself. What say'st thou to him?

EDGAR.   Draw thy sword,

　　That, if my speech offend a noble heart,

　　Thy arm may do thee justice. Here is mine.

　　Behold, it is the privilege of mine honours,

爱德蒙：　吹！（喇叭初响。）

传令官：　再吹！（喇叭再响。）

传令官：　再吹！（喇叭三响。）
　　　　　（内喇叭声相应。）

（喇叭手前导，爱德伽武装上。）

奥本尼：　问明他的来意，为什么他听了喇叭的呼召到这儿来。

传令官：　你是什么人？你叫什么名字？在军中是什么官级？为什么你要应召而来？

爱德伽：　我的名字已经被阴谋的毒齿咬啮蛀蚀了；可是我的出身正像我现在所要来面对的敌手同样高贵。

奥本尼：　谁是你的敌手？
爱德伽：　代表葛罗斯特伯爵爱德蒙的是什么人？
爱德蒙：　他自己；你对他有什么话说？
爱德伽：　拔出你的剑来，要是我的话激怒了一颗正直的心，你的兵器可以为你辩护；这儿是我的剑。听着，虽然你有的是胆量、勇气、权位和尊荣，虽然你挥着胜利的宝剑，夺到了新的幸运，可是凭着我的荣誉、我的誓言和我的骑士的身份所给我的特权，

My oath, and my profession. I protest –
Maugre thy strength, youth, place, and eminence,
Despite thy victor sword and fire-new fortune,
Thy valour and thy heart – thou art a traitor;
False to thy gods, thy brother, and thy father;
Conspirant 'gainst this high illustrious prince;
And from th' extremest upward of thy head
To the descent and dust beneath thy foot,
A most toad-spotted traitor.Say thou no,
This sword, this arm, and my best spirits are bent
To prove upon thy heart, whereto I speak,
Thou liest.

EDMUND.   In wisdom I should ask thy name;
But since thy outside looks so fair and warlike,
And that thy tongue some say of breeding breathes,
What safe and nicely I might well delay
By rule of knighthood, I disdain and spurn.
Back do I toss those treasons to thy head;
With the hell-hated lie o'erwhelm thy heart;
Which – for they yet glance by and scarcely bruise –
This sword of mine shall give them instant way
Where they shall rest for ever. Trumpets, speak!
[*Alarums. They fight. Edmund falls.*]

DUKE OF ALBANY.   Save him, save him!
GONERIL.   This is mere practice, Gloster.

我当众宣布你是一个叛徒，不忠于你的神明、你的兄长和你的父亲，阴谋倾覆这一位崇高卓越的君王，从你的头顶直到你的足下的尘土，彻头彻尾是一个最可憎的逆贼。要是你说一声"不"，这一柄剑、这一只胳臂和我的全身的勇气，都要向你的心口证明你说谎。

爱德蒙：　　照理我应该问你的名字；可是你的外表既然这样英勇，你的出言吐语，也可以表明你不是一个卑微的人，虽然按照骑士的规则，我可以拒绝你的挑战，我却不惜唾弃这些规则，把你所说的那种罪名仍旧丢回到你的头上，让那像地狱一般可憎的谎话吞没你的心；凭着这一柄剑，我要在你的心头挖破一个窟窿，把你的罪恶一起塞进去。吹起来，喇叭！（号角声。二人决斗。爱德蒙倒地。）

奥本尼：　　留他活命，留他活命！
高纳里尔：　　这是诡计，葛罗斯特；按照决斗的法律，你尽可以不

By th' law of arms thou wast not bound to answer

An unknown opposite. Thou art not vanquished,

But cozened and beguiled.

DUKE OF ALBANY.　Shut your mouth, dame,

Or with this paper shall I stop it. – Hold, sir.

Thou worse than any name, read thine own evil.

No tearing, lady! I perceive you know it.

[*Gives the letter to Edmund.*]

GONERIL.　Say if I do – the laws are mine, not thine.

Who can arraign me for't?

DUKE OF ALBANY.　Most monstrous!

Know'st thou this paper?

GONERIL.　Ask me not what I know.

[*Exit.*]

DUKE OF ALBANY.　Go after her. She's desperate; govern her.

[*Exit an Officer.*]

EDMUND.　What, you have charged me with, that have I done,

And more, much more. The time will bring it out.

'Tis past, and so am I.– But what art thou

That hast this fortune on me? If thou'rt noble,

I do forgive thee.

EDGAR.　Let's exchange charity.

I am no less in blood than thou art, Edmund;

If more, the more th' hast wronged me.

My name is Edgar and thy father's son.

The gods are just, and of our pleasant vices

接受一个不知名的对手的挑战；你不是被人打败，你是中了人家的计了。

奥本尼： 闭住你的嘴，妇人，否则我要用这一张纸塞住它了。且慢，骑士。你这比一切恶名更恶的恶人，读读你自己的罪恶吧。不要撕，太太；我看你也认识这一封信的。（以信授爱德蒙。）

高纳里尔： 即使我认识这一封信，又有什么关系！法律在我手中，不在你手中；谁可以控诉我？

奥本尼： 岂有此理！你知道这封信吗？

高纳里尔： 不要问我知道不知道。（下。）

奥本尼： 追上她去；她现在情急了，什么事都干得出来；留心看着她。（一军官下。）

爱德蒙： 你所指斥我的罪状，我全都承认；而且我所干的事，着实不止这一些呢，总有一天会全部暴露的。现在这些事已成过去，我也要永辞人世了。——可是你是什么人，我会失败在你的手里？假如你是一个贵族，我愿意对你不记仇恨。

爱德伽： 让我们互相宽恕吧。在血统上我并不比你低微，爱德蒙；要是我的出身比你更高贵，你尤其不该那样陷害我。我的名字是爱德伽，你的父亲的儿子。公正的天神使我们的风流罪过成为惩罚我们的工具；他在黑暗淫邪的地方生下了你，结果使他丧失了他的眼睛。

Make instruments to scourge us.

The dark and vicious place where thee he got

Cost him his eyes.

EDMUND.   Th' hast spoken right; 'tis true.

The wheel is come full circle; I am here.

DUKE OF ALBANY.   Methought thy very gait did prophesy

A royal nobleness. I must embrace thee.

Let sorrow split my heart if ever I

Did hate thee, or thy father!

EDGAR.   Worthy prince, I know't.

DUKE OF ALBANY.   Where have you hid yourself?

How have you known the miseries of your father?

EDGAR.   By nursing them, my lord. List a brief tale;

And when 'tis told, O that my heart would burst!

The bloody proclamation to escape

That followed me so near O, our lives' sweetness!

That with the pain of death would hourly die

Rather than die at once! taught me to shift

Into a madman's rags, t' assume a semblance

That very dogs disdained; and in this habit

Met I my father with his bleeding rings,

Their precious stones new lost; became his guide,

Led him, begged for him, saved him from despair;

Never O fault! revealed myself unto him

Until some half hour past, when I was armed,

Not sure, though hoping of this good success,

爱德蒙：　你说得不错；天道的车轮已经循环过来了。

奥本尼：　我一看见你的举止行动，就觉得你不是一个凡俗之人。我必须拥抱你；让悔恨碎裂了我的心，要是我曾经憎恨过你和你的父亲。

爱德伽：　殿下，我一向知道您的仁慈。

奥本尼：　你把自己藏匿在什么地方？你怎么知道你的父亲的灾难？

爱德伽：　殿下，我知道他的灾难，因为我就在他的身边照料他，听我讲一段简短的故事；当我说完以后，啊，但愿我的心爆裂了吧！贪生怕死，是我们人类的常情，我们宁愿每小时忍受着死亡的惨痛，也不愿一下子结束自己的生命；我为了逃避那紧迫着我的、残酷的宣判，不得不披上一身疯人的褴褛衣服，改扮成一副连狗儿们也要看不起的样子。在这样的乔装之中，我碰见了我的父亲，他的两个眼眶里淋着血，那宝贵的眼珠已经失去了；我替他做向导，带着他走路，为他向人求乞，把他从绝望之中拯救出来；啊！千不该、万不该，我不该向他瞒住我自己的真相！直到约摸半小时以前，我已经披上甲胄，虽说希望天从人愿，却不知道此行究竟结果如何，便请他为我祝福，才把我的全部经历从头到尾告诉他知道；可是唉！他的破碎的心太脆弱了，载不起这样重大的喜悦和悲伤，在这两种极端的情绪猛烈的冲突之下，他含着微笑死了。

I asked his blessing, and from first to last

Told him my pilgrimage. But his flawed heart

Alack, too weak the conflict to support!

Twixt two extremes of passion, joy and grief,

Burst smilingly.

EDMUND.　This speech of yours hath moved me,

And shall perchance do good; but speak you on;

You look as you had something more to say.

DUKE OF ALBANY.　If there be more, more woful, hold it in;

For I am almost ready to dissolve,

Hearing of this.

EDGAR.　This would have seemed a period

To such as love not sorrow; but another,

To amplify too much, would make much more,

And top extremity.

Whilst I was big in clamour, came there a man,

Who, having seen me in my worst estate,

Shunned my abhorred society; but then, finding

Who 'twas that so endured, with his strong arms

He fastened on my neck, and bellowed out

As heed burst heaven; threw him on my father;

Told the most piteous tale of Lear and him

That ever ear received; which in recounting

His grief grew puissant, and the strings of life

Began to crack. Twice then the trumpets sounded,

And there I left him tranced.

爱德蒙：　　你这番话很使我感动，说不定对我有好处；可是说下去吧，看上去你还有一些话要说。

奥本尼：　　要是还有比这更伤心的事，请不要说下去了吧；因为我听了这样的话，已经忍不住热泪盈眶了。

爱德伽：　　对于不喜欢悲哀的人，这似乎已经是悲哀的顶点；可是在极度的悲哀之上，却还有更大的悲哀。当我正在放声大哭的时候，来了一个人，他认识我就是他所见过的那个疯丐，不敢接近我；可是后来他知道了我究竟是什么人，遭遇到什么样不幸，他就抱住我的头颈，大放悲声，好像要把天空都震碎一般；他俯伏在我的父亲的尸体上；讲出了关于李尔和他两个人的一段最凄惨的故事；他越讲越伤心，他的生命之弦都要开始颤断了；那时候喇叭的声音已经响过二次，我只好抛下他一个人在那如痴如醉的状态之中。

DUKE OF ALBANY.　But who was this?

EDGAR.　Kent, sir, the banished Kent; who in disguise

　　Followed his enemy king and did him service

　　Improper for a slave.

[*Enter a Gentleman with a bloody knife.*]

GENTLEMAN.　Help, help! O, help!

EDGAR.　What kind of help?

DUKE OF ALBANY.　Speak, man.

EDGAR.　What means that bloody knife?

GENTLEMAN.　'Tis hot, it smokes.

　　It came even from the heart of

　　– O! she's dead!

DUKE OF ALBANY.　Who dead? Speak, man.

GENTLEMAN.　Your lady, sir, your lady! and her sister

　　By her is poisoned; she hath confessed it.

EDMUND.　I was contracted to them both.

　　All three

　　Now marry in an instant.

EDGAR.　Here comes Kent.

DUKE OF ALBANY.　Produce their bodies, be they alive or dead.

　　This judgement of the heavens, that makes us tremble

　　Touches us not with pity.

　　[*Exit Gentleman.*]

　　[*Enter Kent.*]

奥本尼：　可是这是什么人？

爱德伽：　肯特，殿下，被放逐的肯特；他一路上乔装改貌，跟随那把他视同仇敌的国王，替他躬操奴隶不如的贱役。

（一侍臣持一流血之刀上。）

侍臣：　救命！救命！救命啊！

爱德伽：　救什么命！

奥本尼：　说呀，什么事？

爱德伽：　那柄血淋淋的刀是什么意思？

侍臣：　它还热腾腾地冒着气呢；它是从她的心窝里拔出来的，——啊！她死了！

奥本尼：　谁死了？说呀。

侍臣：　您的夫人，殿下，您的夫人；她的妹妹也给她毒死了，她自己承认的。

爱德蒙：　我跟她们两人都有婚姻之约，现在我们三个人可以在一块儿做夫妻了。

爱德伽：　肯特来了。

奥本尼：　把她们的尸体抬出来，不管她们有没有死。这一个上天的判决使我们战栗，却不能引起我们的怜悯。（侍臣下。）

（肯特上。）啊！这就是他吗？当前的变故使我不能对他尽我应尽的敬礼。

O, is this he?

The time will not allow the compliment

That very manners urges.

EARL OF KENT.　I am come

To bid my king and master aye good night.

Is he not here?

DUKE OF ALBANY.　Great thing of us forgot!

Speak, Edmund, where's the King? and where's Cordelia?

[*The bodies of Goneril and Regan are brought in.*]

Seest thou this object, Kent?

EARL OF KENT.　Alack, why thus?

EDMUND.　Yet Edmund was beloved.

The one the other poisoned for my sake,

And after slew herself.

DUKE OF ALBANY.　Even so. Cover their faces.

EDMUND.　I pant for life. Some good I mean to do,

Despite of mine own nature. Quickly send

Be brief in't to the castle; for my writ

Is on the life of Lear and on Cordelia.

Nay, send in time.

DUKE OF ALBANY.　Run, run, O, run!

EDGAR.　To who, my lord? Who has the office? Send

Thy token of reprieve.

EDMUND.　Well thought on. Take my sword;

Give it the Captain.

DUKE OF ALBANY.　Haste thee for thy life.

肯特：　　我要来向我的王上道一声永久的晚安，他不在这儿吗？

奥本尼：　我们把一件重要的事情忘了！爱德蒙，王上呢？考狄利娅呢？（侍从抬高纳里尔、里根二尸体上。）肯特，你看见这一种情景吗？

肯特：　　哎哟！这是为了什么？

爱德蒙：　爱德蒙还是有人爱的；这一个为了我的缘故毒死了那一个，跟着她也自杀了。

奥本尼：　正是这样。把她们的脸遮起来。

爱德蒙：　我快要断气了，倒想做一件违反我的本性的好事。赶快差人到城堡里去，因为我已经下令，要把李尔和考狄利娅处死。不要多说废话，迟一点就来不及啦。

奥本尼：　跑！跑！跑呀！

爱德伽：　跑去找谁呀，殿下？——谁奉命干这件事的？你得给我一件什么东西，作为赦免的凭证。

爱德蒙：　想得不错；把我的剑拿去给那队长。

奥本尼：　快去，快去。（爱德伽下。）

[*Exit Edgar.*]

EDMUND.　He hath commission from thy wife and me

　　To hang Cordelia in the prison and

　　To lay the blame upon her own despair

　　That she fordid herself.

DUKE OF ALBANY.　The gods defend her! Bear him hence awhile.

　　[*Edmund is borne off.*]

[*Enter Lear, with Cordelia dead in his arms; Edgar, Officer, and others .*]

KING LEAR.　Howl, howl, howl, howl! O, you are men of stone.

　　Had I your tongues and eyes, I'ld use them so

　　That heaven's vault should crack. She's gone for ever!

　　I know when one is dead, and when one lives.

　　She's dead as earth. Lend me a looking glass.

　　If that her breath will mist or stain the stone,

　　Why, then she lives.

EARL OF KENT.　Is this the promised end?

EDGAR.　Or image of that horror?

DUKE OF ALBANY.　Fall and cease!

KING LEAR.　This feather stirs; she lives! If it be so,

　　It is a chance which does redeem all sorrows

　　That ever I have felt.

EARL OF KENT.　[*Kneeling.*] O my good master!

爱德蒙：　　他从我的妻子跟我两人的手里得到密令，要把考狄利娅在狱中缢死，对外面说是她自己在绝望中自杀的。

奥本尼：　　神明保佑她！把他暂时抬出去。（侍从抬爱德蒙下。）

（李尔抱考狄利娅尸体，爱德伽、军官及余人等同上。）

李尔：　　哀号吧，哀号吧，哀号吧，哀号吧！啊！你们都是些石头一样的人；要是我有了你们的那些舌头和眼睛，我要用我的眼泪和哭声震撼穹苍。她是一去不回的了。一个人死了还是活着，我是知道的；她已经像泥土一样死去。借一面镜子给我；要是她的气息还能够在镜面上呵起一层薄雾，那么她还没有死。

肯特：　　这就是世界最后的结局吗？

爱德伽：　　还是末日恐怖的预兆？

奥本尼：　　天倒下来了，一切都要归于毁灭吗？

李尔：　　这一根羽毛在动；她没有死！要是她还有活命，那么我的一切悲哀都可以消释了。

肯特：　　（跪。）啊，我的好主人！

KING LEAR. Prithee away!

EDGAR. 'Tis noble Kent, your friend.

KING LEAR. A plague upon you, murderers, traitors all!

I might have saved her; now she's gone for ever!

Cordelia, Cordelia! stay a little. Ha!

What is't thou say'st, Her voice was ever soft,

Gentle, and low – an excellent thing in woman.

I killed the slave that was a-hanging thee.

OFFICER. 'Tis true, my lords, he did.

KING LEAR. Did I not, fellow?

I have seen the day, with my good biting falchion

I would have made them skip. I am old now,

And these same crosses spoil me. Who are you?

Mine eyes are not o' th' best. I'll tell you straight.

EARL OF KENT. If fortune brag of two she loved and hated,

One of them we behold.

KING LEAR. This' a dull sight. Are you not Kent?

EARL OF KENT. The same –

Your servant Kent. Where is your servant Caius?

KING LEAR. He's a good fellow, I can tell you that.

He'll strike, and quickly too. He's dead and rotten.

EARL OF KENT. No, my good lord; I am the very man –

KING LEAR. I'll see that straight.

EARL OF KENT. That from your first of difference and decay

Have followed your sad steps.

KING LEAR. You're welcome hither.

李尔：　　走开！

爱德伽：　　这是尊贵的肯特，您的朋友。

李尔：　　一场瘟疫降落在你们身上，全是些凶手，奸贼！我本来可以把她救活的；现在她再也回不转来了！考狄利娅，考狄利娅！等一等。嘿！你说什么？她的声音总是那么柔软温和，女儿家是应该这样的。我亲手杀死了那把你缢死的奴才。

军官：　　殿下，他真的把他杀死了。

李尔：　　我不是把他杀死了吗，汉子？从前我一举起我的宝刀，就可以叫他们吓得抱头鼠窜；现在年纪老啦，受到这许多磨难，一天比一天不中用啦。你是谁？等会儿我就可以说出来了；我的眼睛可不大好。

肯特：　　要是命运女神向人夸口，说起有两个曾经一度被她宠爱、后来却为她厌弃的人，那么在我们的眼前就各站着其中的一个。

李尔：　　我的眼睛太糊涂啦。你不是肯特吗？

肯特：　　正是，您的仆人肯特。您的仆人卡厄斯呢？

李尔：　　他是一个好人，我可以告诉你；他一动起火来就会打人。他现在已经死得骨头都腐烂了。

肯特：　　不，陛下；我就是那个人——

李尔：　　我马上能认出来你是不是。

肯特：　　自从您开始遭遇变故以来，一直跟随着您的不幸的足迹。

李尔：　　欢迎，欢迎。

EARL OF KENT.   Nor no man else! All's cheerless, dark, and deadly.

Your eldest daughters have fordone themselves,

And desperately are dead.

KING LEAR.   Ay, so I think.

DUKE OF ALBANY.   He knows not what he says; and vain is it

That we present us to him.

EDGAR.   Very bootless.

[*Enter an Officer.*]

OFFICER.   Edmund is dead, my lord.

DUKE OF ALBANY.   That's but a trifle here.

You lords and noble friends, know our intent.

What comfort to this great decay may come

Shall be applied. For us, we will resign,

During the life of this old Majesty,

To him our absolute power;

[*To Edgar and Kent.*] you to your rights;

With boot, and Such addition as your honours

Have more than merited. – All friends shall taste

The wages of their virtue, and all foes

The cup of their deservings. – O, see, see!

KING LEAR.   And my poor fool is hanged! No, no, no life!

Why should a dog, a horse, a rat, have life,

And thou no breath at all? Thou'lt come no more,

Never, never, never, never, never!

肯特：　不，一切都是凄惨的、黑暗的、阴郁的。您的两个大女儿已经在绝望中自杀了。

李尔：　嗯，我也想是这样的。

奥本尼：　他不知道他自己在说些什么话，我们谒见他也是徒然的。

爱德伽：　全然是徒劳。

（一军官上。）

军官：　启禀殿下，爱德蒙死了。

奥本尼：　他的死在现在不过是一件无足重轻的小事。各位勋爵和尊贵的朋友，听我向你们宣示我的旨意：对于这一位老病衰弱的君王，我们将要尽我们的力量给他可能的安慰；当他在世的时候，我仍旧把最高的权力归还给他。（向爱德伽、肯特）你们两位仍旧恢复原来的爵位，我还要加赉你们额外的尊荣，褒扬你们过人的节行。一切朋友都要得到他们忠贞的报酬，一切仇敌都要尝到他们罪恶的苦杯。——啊！瞧，瞧！

李尔：　我的可怜的傻瓜给他们缢死了！不，不，没有命了！为什么一条狗、一匹马、一只耗子，都有它们的生命，你却没有一丝呼吸？你是永不回来的了，永不，永不，永不，永不，永不！请你替我解开这个纽扣；谢谢你，先生。你看见吗？瞧着她，

Pray you undo this button. Thank you, sir.

Do you see this? Look on her! look!her lips!

Look there, look there!

[*He dies.*]

EDGAR.　He faints! My lord, my lord!

EARL OF KENT.　Break, heart; I prithee break!

EDGAR.　Look up, my lord.

EARL OF KENT.　Vex not his ghost. O, let him pass! He hates him

That would upon the rack of this tough world

Stretch him out longer.

EDGAR.　He is gone indeed.

EARL OF KENT.　The wonder is, he hath endured so long.

He but usurped his life.

DUKE OF ALBANY.　Bear them from hence. Our present business Is

general woe.

[*To Kent and Edgar.*] Friends of my soul, you twain

Rule in this realm, and the gored state sustain.

EARL OF KENT.　I have a journey, sir, shortly to go.

My master calls me; I must not say no.

DUKE OF ALBANY.　The weight of this sad time we must obey,

Speak what we feel, not what we ought to say.

The oldest have borne most; we that are young

Shall never see so much, nor live so long.

[*Exeunt, with a dead march.*]

(THE END)

瞧，她的嘴唇，瞧那边，瞧那边！（死。）

爱德伽：　他晕过去了！——陛下，陛下！

肯特：　碎吧，心啊！碎吧！

爱德伽：　抬起头来，陛下。

肯特：　不要烦扰他的灵魂。啊！让他安然死去吧；他将要痛恨那
想要使他在这无情的人世多受一刻酷刑的人。

爱德伽：　他真的去了。

肯特：　他居然忍受了这么久的时候，才是一件奇事；他的生命不
是他自己的。

奥本尼：　把他们抬出去。我们现在要传令全国举哀。（向肯特、
爱德伽）两位朋友，帮我主持大政，培养这已经斫伤的国本。

肯特：　不日间我就要登程上道；我已经听见主上的呼召。

奥本尼：　不幸的重担不能不肩负；
感情是我们唯一的言语。
年老的人已经忍受一切，
后人只有抚陈迹而叹息。（同下。奏丧礼进行曲。）

（完）

中英对照全译本系列书目表

英国文学卷

《简爱》

《傲慢与偏见》

《理智与情感》

《爱玛》

《金银岛》

《呼啸山庄》

《双城记》

《雾都孤儿》

《柳林风声》

《鲁滨逊漂流记》

《一九八四 动物庄园》

《福尔摩斯经典探案集 血字的研究 四签名》

《福尔摩斯经典探案集 巴斯克维尔的猎犬 恐怖谷》

《福尔摩斯经典探案集 福尔摩斯历险记》

《福尔摩斯经典探案集 福尔摩斯回忆录》

《福尔摩斯经典探案集 福尔摩斯归来记》

《福尔摩斯经典探案集 最后的致意》

《福尔摩斯经典探案集 福尔摩斯新探案集》

《培根散文集》

《德伯家的苔丝》

《格列佛游记》

《道林·格雷的画像》

《消失的地平线》

《艰难时世》

美国文学卷

《红字》

《小妇人》

《伟大的盖茨比》

《瓦尔登湖》

《房龙地理》

《纯真年代》

《秘密花园》

《嘉莉妹妹》

《人类的故事》

《老人与海》

《太阳照常升起》

《乞力马扎罗的雪 海明威短篇小说选》

《哈克贝利·费恩历险记》